AF679239

Export Essentials
Pulse Trade Data

June 2014

Export Essentials
Pulse Trade Data

Liam Clancey, Editor

Copyright © 2014 by STAT Publishing

Cover by: The White Rock Design Crew

All rights reserved. No part of this book may be reproduced in any form by any electronic or mechanical means including photocopying, recording, or information storage and retrieval without permission in writing from STAT Publishing.

Information has been obtained from sources believed to be reliable. However, STAT Publishing does not guarantee the accuracy, adequacy or completeness of any information and/or recommendations contained herein, and is not responsible for nor liable for any results obtained from their use.

Cover photograph is copyright © 2014 iStockphoto.com/Jonathan (http://www.istockphoto.com/jono0001). The photograph is being used by permission of the photographer under the standard license agreement.

ISBN-978-1-895412-15-4

Book Website
www.statpub.com/books
Email: editor@statpub.com

Give feedback on the book at:
feedback@statpub.com

Printed in U.S.A.

Contents

Introduction

For much of the past couple of years tight supplies of key pulses have strongly influenced price direction. For the coming year, markets expect to see more power returned to the hands of buyers as available supplies of pulses.

However, there is an underlying worry that weather conditions could cause major damage to crops in a key producing or consuming region of the world.

If there are no significant problems, global production of dry edible beans, lentils, field peas and chickpeas could reach a record 52.75 million metric tons across the entire 2014-15 marketing year. If realized, output would be up 2.9% over last season and 6.6% above the recent five year average.

Production of all classes of pulses are expected to rise, with lentils potentially jumping 11.1% to 4.23 million metric tons, while world field pea output may climb just 1.9% to 11.33 million. Dry edible beans are the most important category of pulses grown in the world. Global production is expected to rise 2.9% in the coming year to 23.77 million metric tons. Chickpeas are the second most commonly grown in the pulse in the world, reflecting massive production of desi type chickpeas in India. Global output of desi and kabuli chickpeas could jump 5.8% to 13.41 million metric tons in 2014-15.

As good as the world supply situation looks on paper, markets are nervous. Prospects for an El Nino event this year has put importers on the Indian subcontinent on edge because it can contribute to below normal monsoon rainfall. Last year's monsoon rains were above normal.

While they had little positive impact on the 2013 kharif crop, they seem to have given rabi season crops a big boost. In its Third Advance Estimates, India's agriculture department said it believes output of all pulses will reach a record 19.57 million metric tons during 2013-14. There is no reason to believe that production will remain this high in the coming season, with the potential for output to drop under 18.74 million metric ton in the coming year.

Despite harvesting record quantities of pulses in 2013-14, India still needed to import over three million metric tons of product from all over the world. In the past, it was believed India needed 17.5 kilograms of pulses per person per year to meet their minimum daily dietary needs. By that measure, India was chronically short of pulses prior to 2012. Significantly, India has never grown enough pulses to cover that minimum dietary need.

More recently, dietitians have argued the actual requirement is closer to 20 kilograms per capita. Imports plus production have never been high enough to cover that estimated requirement. India's imports are expected to rise in 2014-15. An El Nino event and problems with the monsoon could see that number grow.

In recent years, China has also emerged as a powerful force on global pulse markets. It is one of the largest exporters of dry edible beans, particularly kidney type. Last year's crop failure contributed to bullish market conditions for colored beans, extending the fundamental shortage of product which started with Argentina's 2013 drought and the failure of its black and white alubia bean crops. Edible bean fundamentals are expected to improve significantly as production in both countries rebounds.

China is also one of the world's largest field pea importers. Demand was initially driven by noodle manufacturers. In more recent years, other food manufacturers in China have been exploring uses for whole and fractioned peas as well as flour. Similar expansion is underway in other parts of the world, bringing with it to the potential to increase base demand for whole peas. China's importers expect purchases during the last half of 2014 to again set a new record this calendar year.

One effect of the recent gains in pulse production in India and expanded uses for pulses in food products is that global per capita pulse consumption has stopped declining for the time being. It remains below levels recorded during the first half of the 20th century, but is moving in a positive direction as the world prepares for the Year of Pulses in 2016.

Fundamental Statistics Overview

India – Pulse Supply-Demand Forecast

(hectares, metric tons)

Production	Season	2010-11	2011-12	2012-13	2013-14
Tur	Kharif	2,860,000	2,650,000	3,020,000	3,380,000
Gram	Rabi	8,220,000	7,700,000	8,830,000	9,930,000
Urad	Kharif	1,400,000	1,230,000	1,430,000	1,180,000
	Rabi	360,000	540,000	470,000	320,000
	Total	1,760,000	1,770,000	1,900,000	1,500,000
Moong	Kharif	1,530,000	1,240,000	790,000	970,000
	Rabi	290,000	390,000	400,000	430,000
	Total	1,820,000	1,630,000	1,190,000	1,400,000
Other	Kharif	1,330,000	940,000	620,000	760,000
	Rabi	2,250,000	2,400,000	2,730,000	2,600,000
	Total	3,580,000	3,340,000	3,350,000	3,360,000
All Pulses	Kharif	7,120,000	6,060,000	5,860,000	6,290,000
	Rabi	11,120,000	11,030,000	12,430,000	13,280,000
Total Production	Total	18,240,000	17,090,000	18,290,000	19,570,000
				18,290,000	19,570,000
Pulse Imports	Peas	2,029,000	1,457,000	1,691,000	1,251,000
	Chickpeas	106,000	244,000	677,000	455,000
	Lentils	177,000	259,000	793,000	599,000
	Beans	837,000	1,067,000	1,272,000	946,000
Total Imports	All Pulses	3,149,000	3,027,000	4,433,000	3,251,000
Available Supply and Inferred Consumption (production plus imports)					
Total Supply	Pulses	21,389,000	20,117,000	22,723,000	22,821,000

Production estimates and forecasts based on historical data from India's agriculture department. Trade estimates based on data from exporting nations and the FAO.

Canada – Specialty Crop Production Summary

(acres, metric tons, pounds per acre)

Area (acres)	2010	2011	2012	2013	2014
Lentils	3,445,000	2,557,800	2,515,000	2,393,000	2,860,000
Dry Peas	3,625,000	2,436,700	3,730,000	3,285,000	3,975,000
Edible Beans	331,100	197,881	305,000	241,000	293,000
Chick Peas	205,000	117,500	200,000	180,000	100,000
Canaryseed	395,000	275,000	335,000	210,000	245,000
Mustard	470,000	327,958	335,000	365,000	480,000
Sunflower	135,000	35,000	100,000	70,000	125,000
Soybean	3,738,800	3,851,662	4,152,900	4,518,900	5,264,000
Production (MT)	2010	2011	2012	2013	2014
Lentils	2,004,800	1,573,500	1,537,900	1,880,500	1,844,000
Dry Peas	3,018,200	2,502,000	3,340,500	3,849,300	3,835,000
Edible Beans	253,600	162,400	274,300	206,100	240,000
Chick Peas	128,300	85,600	161,400	169,400	77,000
Canaryseed	153,500	128,600	149,700	131,000	121,000
Mustard	182,000	130,000	118,600	154,500	189,000
Sunflower	67,600	19,800	86,900	51,900	83,000
Soybean	4,444,600	4,297,700	5,086,400	5,198,400	6,017,000
Yields (lbs)	2010	2011	2012	2013	2014
Lentils	1,283	1,356	1,348	1,732	1,421
Dry Peas	1,836	2,264	1,974	2,583	2,127
Edible Beans	1,689	1,809	1,983	1,885	1,806
Chick Peas	1,380	1,606	1,779	2,075	1,698
Canaryseed	857	1,031	985	1,375	1,089
Mustard	854	874	780	933	868
Sunflower	1,104	1,247	1,916	1,635	1,464
Soybean	2,621	2,460	2,700	2,536	2,520

BASED on Statistics Canada data. Copyright 2014 STAT Communications Ltd., Canada.

Canadian Specialty Grain Export Summary April, 2014

(metric tons)

Crop Year	2011-12	2012-13	2012-13	2013-14	2014
Period	Aug-Jul	Aug-Jul	Aug-Apr	Aug-Apr	Apr
Yellow Pea	1,730,321	2,296,084	1,723,437	1,549,735	42,871
Green Pea	237,947	171,164	154,710	231,961	16,256
Split Pea	87,544	118,553	95,608	89,202	27,109
Whole & Split Pea	2,098,929	2,654,515	2,024,983	1,957,330	99,041
Green Lentil	540,828	725,716	490,827	499,840	64,214
Red Lentil	557,984	889,905	620,868	697,622	57,882
Lentil	1,148,004	1,639,046	1,130,795	1,217,590	124,180
Kabuli Chickpea	24,506	59,815	46,596	21,636	4,148
Chickpea	38,154	71,633	56,309	26,896	4,916
Navy or Pea Bean	75,560	105,016	80,909	94,613	9,455
Kidney & Navy Bean	104,138	125,261	96,253	112,618	10,944
Pinto Bean	25,483	58,909	48,165	32,300	5,217
Small Red Bean	14,465	14,549	11,028	13,296	1,448
Mung Bean	2,278	2,606	1,933	2,154	141
Fababean	2,444	2,473	2,029	8,013	1,292
Bambara Bean	0	0	0	2	0
Cowpea	132	281	0	17	10
Pigeon Pea	6	63	62	27	23
Bean (nes)	103,445	154,215	129,992	112,316	10,566
Canaryseed	126,385	136,236	98,114	113,689	13,522
Millet	4,787	4,603	3,597	2,840	380
Buckwheat	4,091	3,775	2,858	2,930	756
Mustard Seed	115,186	120,108	90,036	101,027	11,824
Sunflower	33,343	43,752	31,476	37,938	5,078
Canola	8,695,179	7,113,875	5,905,727	6,509,853	976,148
Linseed (flax)	390,462	481,537	341,673	414,773	49,860
Soybean	3,622,382	3,470,417	3,082,106	2,872,600	117,546
Safflower Seed	173	570	348	282	15
Coriander Seed	4,577	4,405	3,468	4,433	383
Cumin Seed	45	58	40	72	7
Caraway Seed	87	1	0	4	0
Minor Oilseed	2,968	4,074	2,495	4,328	729

Source Statistics Canada

U.S. Specialty Grain Export Summary April, 2014

(metric tons)

Crop Year	2011-12	2012-13	2012-13	2013-14	2014
Period	Sep-Aug	Sep-Aug	Sep-Apr	Sep-Apr	Apr
Pinto Bean	133,330	103,794	72,146	43,679	4,200
Black Bean	65,575	54,140	36,457	19,324	2,216
Pea Bean	104,382	115,777	71,242	143,568	17,632
Great Northern Bean	20,486	35,420	26,074	30,930	3,291
Dark Red Kidney Bean	16,975	27,290	20,654	28,813	2,305
Light Red Kidney Bean	5,702	3,423	2,165	3,409	128
Kidney (nes)	37,242	54,109	39,317	25,261	3,656
Small Red Bean	8,888	10,067	6,367	10,187	1,662
Pink Bean	1,569	1,257	968	578	48
Cranberry Bean	3,518	2,036	1,708	5,356	805
Mung Bean	11,034	6,458	5,498	4,474	529
Small White Bean	660	1,295	1,129	802	370
Baby Lima Bean	3,663	5,082	3,283	5,549	932
Large Lima Bean	12,329	15,713	10,587	11,481	2,776
Blackeye Cowpea	22,594	9,090	6,596	2,405	120
Broadbean	535	4,998	1,721	9,155	1,429
Pigeon Pea	53	28	10	12	5
Bambara Bean	16	78	49	44	12
Bean (nes)	20,209	23,047	17,542	16,161	2,191
Lentil	171,524	231,780	175,959	105,732	18,940
Green Pea	105,256	110,179	88,301	134,571	9,755
Yellow Pea	66,520	52,689	37,109	102,019	5,785
Split Pea	81,908	74,253	55,189	44,677	3,516
Aust. Winter Pea	793	4,516	2,947	636	0
Pea (nes)	55,005	44,013	32,266	55,016	4,939
Chickpea	79,325	65,825	57,935	37,515	3,575
Millet	53,953	11,618	9,023	42,270	6,180
Canaryseed	714	1,317	1,177	101	0
Nigerseed	61	61	61	74	0
Popcorn	102,374	99,416	68,987	82,398	13,366
Microwave Popcorn	45,103	47,892	31,993	33,279	4,810
Hulled Sunflower	16,697	12,504	7,705	7,085	814
Confection Sunflower	58,032	81,746	54,591	40,834	6,736
Oil Sunflower	40,632	40,381	31,824	21,130	1,868
Buckwheat	28,600	26,486	14,662	9,252	1,196
Mustard Seed	1,554	2,045	1,284	2,259	319
Melon Seed	645	203	203	0	0
Poppy Seed	65	162	123	64	0

Source U.S. Department of Commerce

Australian Specialty Grain Export Summary April, 2014

(metric tons)

Crop Year Period	2011-12 Nov-Oct	2012-13 Nov-Oct	2012-13 Nov-Apr	2013-14 Nov-Apr	2014 Apr
Whole Pea	169,947	135,284	82,820	67,490	17,522
Split Pea	34,713	31,981	15,948	18,858	2,827
Chickpea	580,138	853,121	666,673	349,242	76,930
Broadbean (faba)	293,539	303,343	232,973	291,914	21,689
Mung Bean	93,984	61,023	12,670	13,566	3,057
Kidney Bean	6	40	17	17	14
Adzuki Bean	1,021	1,527	1,179	648	92
Beans (nes)	379	571	483	150	1
Lentil	381,927	299,627	147,614	194,445	33,818
Vetch, Forage	18,331	4,821	2,554	2,509	400
Millet	23,515	23,468	1,659	12,666	39
Safflower Seed	2,682	1,669	1,233	367	162
Sunflower	948	725	404	235	5
Canaryseed	337	186	53	11	0
Mustard Seed	22	111	96	83	0
Rapeseed	11,765	44,241	19,518	49,077	2,235
Soybean	1,692	8,319	1,476	1,564	42
Linseed (flax)	16	37	26	18	4
Buckwheat	363	104	14	36	6

Source Australian Bureau of Statistics

Australia Pulse Production Summary
(hectares, metric tons)

Area (hectares)	2009	2010	2011	2012	2013
Broad Beans	16,300	21,000	23,000	24,000	27,000
Chickpea All	369,900	546,500	456,000	574,000	507,000
Desi	331,800	502,300	410,200	502,200	427,550
Kabuli	38,100	44,200	45,800	71,800	79,450
Faba Beans	131,500	144,900	151,300	203,000	152,000
Field Pea All	285,100	295,850	249,000	280,500	245,000
Blue	7,000	N/A	N/A	N/A	N/A
Dun	271,100	270,700	249,000	280,500	245,000
White	7,000	N/A	N/A	N/A	N/A
Lentils	104,000	165,500	172,800	164,400	168,400
Lupin All	485,800	567,900	689,000	450,200	386,850
Albus	40,600	51,400	38,400	30,700	32,850
Angustifolius	445,200	516,500	650,600	419,500	354,000
Mung Beans	80,000	88,000	115,000	85,000	86,000
Navy Beans	3,000	3,000	3,000	3,000	3,000
Vetch	23,399	28,200	28,000	20,000	17,000
All Pulses	1,498,999	1,860,850	1,887,100	1,804,100	1,592,250

Australia Pulse Production Summary
(metric tons)

Production	2009	2010	2011	2012	2013
Production	2009	2010	2011	2012	2013
Broad Beans	17,000	48,100	42,000	47,300	49,600
Chickpea All	512,450	461,710	673,000	813,300	629,000
Desi	475,000	395,380	590,660	735,300	531,000
Kabuli	37,450	66,330	82,340	78,000	98,000
Faba Beans	224,900	286,700	268,100	377,000	328,000
Field Pea All	351,000	427,940	342,000	319,000	342,000
Blue	5,300	N/A	N/A	N/A	N/A
Dun	339,700	427,940	342,000	319,000	342,000
White	6,000	N/A	N/A	N/A	N/A
Lentils	143,000	306,210	307,000	273,500	253,000
Lupin All	611,850	614,400	900,550	458,700	625,000
Albus	47,100	92,290	60,150	34,000	39,900
Angustifolius	564,750	522,110	840,400	424,700	585,100
Mung Beans	92,000	93,000	122,000	87,000	73,100
Navy Beans	2,700	2,600	2,500	3,100	2,800

Australia Pulse Production Summary

(metric tons)

Yield	2009	2010	2011	2012	2013
Vetch	3,895	4,100	5,400	4,500	3,400
All Pulses	1,958,795	2,244,760	2,662,550	2,383,400	2,305,900
Yield	2009	2010	2011	2012	2013
Broad Beans	1,043	2,290	1,826	1,971	1,837
Chickpea All	1,385	845	1,476	1,417	1,241
Desi	1,432	787	1,440	1,464	1,242
Kabuli	983	1,501	1,798	1,086	1,233
Faba Beans	1,710	1,979	1,772	1,857	2,158
Field Pea All	1,231	1,446	1,373	1,137	1,396
Blue	757	N/A	N/A	N/A	N/A
Dun	1,253	1,581	1,373	1,137	1,396
White	857	N/A	N/A	N/A	N/A
Lentils	1,375	1,850	1,777	1,664	1,502
Lupin All	1,259	1,082	1,307	1,019	1,616
Albus	1,160	1,796	1,566	1,107	1,215
Angustifolius	1,269	1,011	1,292	1,012	1,653
Mung Beans	1,150	1,057	1,061	1,024	850
Navy Beans	900	867	833	1,033	933
Vetch	166	145	193	225	200

BASED on data from Pulse Australia and ABARES. Estimates for mung, navy beans and vetch by STAT Publishing. 2013 production forecasts basis average yields

Beans

World Edible Bean Supply and Demand Situation

(hectares, metric tons, kilograms)

	2010	2011	2012	2013	2014
Area (hectares)	31,052,000	30,080,000	29,703,000	29,093,000	29,628,000
Yield (kg/ha)	798	757	817	794	807
Production	24,768,000	22,757,000	24,256,000	23,107,000	23,898,000
Carry-in	1,246,000	1,191,000	452,000	899,000	905,000
Supply	26,014,000	23,948,000	24,708,000	24,006,000	24,803,000
Trade	4,297,000	4,330,000	4,511,000	5,273,000	4,834,000
Inferred Use	24,823,000	23,496,000	23,809,000	23,101,000	24,079,000
Ending Stock	1,191,000	452,000	899,000	905,000	724,000
Stock-Use Ratio	4.8%	1.9%	3.8%	3.9%	3.0%
Per Capita Use (kg)	3.622	3.391	3.400	3.263	3.402

Estimates by STAT Publishing based data from the FAO, USDA, Statistics Canada, ABARES, and other entities.

World Dry Bean Production Summary

(hectares, metric tons, kilograms)

Area (hectares)	2010	2011	2012	2013	2014
United States	774,000	493,000	705,000	548,000	682,000
Canada	134,000	80,000	123,000	98,000	119,000
China	911,000	914,000	971,000	1,018,000	1,140,000
Myanmar	3,780,000	4,050,000	4,100,000	4,150,000	4,058,000
Argentina	268,000	248,000	260,000	272,000	300,000
Brazil	3,461,000	3,075,000	3,359,000	3,157,000	3,251,000
Mexico	1,517,000	922,000	1,559,000	1,740,000	1,600,000
Other	20,207,000	20,298,000	18,626,000	18,110,000	18,478,000
Total	31,052,000	30,080,000	29,703,000	29,093,000	29,628,000
Production (MT)	**2010**	**2011**	**2012**	**2013**	**2014**
United States	1,443,000	902,000	1,448,000	1,111,000	1,324,000
Canada	254,000	162,000	274,000	206,000	240,000
China	1,339,000	1,583,000	1,462,000	1,312,000	1,736,000
Myanmar	4,390,000	4,455,000	4,700,000	4,800,000	4,627,000
Argentina	338,000	316,000	260,000	96,000	294,000
Brazil	3,733,000	2,806,000	3,511,000	3,311,000	3,204,000
Mexico	963,000	626,000	1,063,000	1,220,000	1,120,000
Other	12,308,000	11,907,000	11,538,000	11,051,000	11,353,000
Total	24,768,000	22,757,000	24,256,000	23,107,000	23,898,000
Yields (kg per hectare)	**2010**	**2011**	**2012**	**2013**	**2014**
United States	1,864	1,830	2,054	2,027	1,941
Canada	1,896	2,025	2,228	2,102	2,017
China	1,470	1,732	1,506	1,289	1,523
Myanmar	1,161	1,100	1,146	1,157	1,140
Argentina	1,261	1,274	1,000	353	980
Brazil	1,079	913	1,045	1,049	986
Mexico	635	679	682	701	700
Other	609	587	619	610	614
World Yield	798	757	817	794	807

Projections by STAT Market Research based on data from Statistics Canada, ABARE, USDA, FAO

China – Dry Bean and Pulse Supply and Demand Forecast

(hectares, metric tons)

	2009	2010	2011	2012	2013
Area (hectares)	904,140	911,141	914,101	971,000	1,018,000
Yield (kg)	1,647	1,469	1,732	1,506	1,289
Production	1,489,135	1,338,693	1,583,498	1,462,000	1,312,400
Opening Stocks	100,000	160,000	5,000	200,000	100,000
Imports	44,166	98,307	240,000	108,000	119,000
Supply	1,633,301	1,597,000	1,828,498	1,770,000	1,531,400
Disappearance					
Exports	854,873	1,089,384	904,957	1,002,000	883,000
Domestic	618,428	502,615	723,541	668,000	628,400
Total Usage	1,473,301	1,592,000	1,628,498	1,670,000	1,511,400
Ending Stocks	160,000	5,000	200,000	100,000	20,000
Stocks/Use	10.9 %	0.3 %	12.3 %	6.0 %	1.3 %

Projections by STAT Market Reasearch based on FAO, unofficial USDA and Chinese government data

Mexico – Dry Edible Bean Supply-Demand Forecast

(hectares, metric tons)

	2010	2011	2012	2013	2014
Area (hectares)	1,517,000	922,000	1,559,000	1,740,000	1,600,000
Yield (kg/Ha)	635	679	682	701	700
Production	963,000	626,000	1,063,000	1,220,000	1,120,000
Opening Stocks	286,000	183,000	8,000	137,000	246,000
Imports	117,470	104,897	234,433	133,000	135,000
Supply	1,366,470	913,897	1,305,433	1,490,000	1,501,000
Disappearance					
Exports	30,249	37,593	16,879	31,000	31,000
Domestic Use	1,153,221	868,304	1,151,554	1,213,000	1,227,000
Total Usage	1,183,470	905,897	1,168,433	1,244,000	1,258,000
Ending Stocks	183,000	8,000	137,000	246,000	243,000
Stocks/Use	15.5 %	0.9 %	11.7 %	19.8 %	19.3 %

BASED on information from the Mexico's Department of Agriculture and USDA

Kidney Beans

U.S. Dark Red Kidney Bean Supply and Demand Estimates
(metric tons, acres)

Year	2010	2011	2012	2013	2014
Acreage	48,500	48,800	46,200	46,700	55,700
Yield (lbs)	1,718	1,619	1,959	1,788	1,793
Production	37,785	35,834	41,051	37,875	45,298
Carryin	8,000	7,500	1,000	100	100
Stocks	45,785	43,334	42,050	37,975	45,398
Disappearance					
Europe	8,212	8,234	21,362	24,600	14,400
Americas	2,225	6,923	3,674	4,100	4,100
Other	2,958	5,817	6,333	1,000	4,300
Total Exports	13,395	20,974	31,369	29,700	22,800
Domestic	22,517	19,011	8,143	5,014	16,271
Seed, Feed, Waste	2,374	2,349	2,439	3,161	2,926
Total Usage	38,285	42,334	41,951	37,875	41,997
Ending Stocks	7,500	1,000	100	100	3,400
Stocks/Use Ratio	19.6 %	2.4 %	0.2 %	0.3 %	8.1 %

Forecasts by STAT Market Research based on data from the USDA and U.S. Department of Commerce

U.S. Light Red Kidney Bean Supply and Demand Estimates

(metric tons, acres)

Year	2010	2011	2012	2013	2014
Acreage	53,100	37,200	40,200	43,200	46,400
Yield (lbs)	1,819	1,726	1,995	1,956	1,881
Production	43,817	29,121	36,378	38,329	39,596
Carryin	5,000	6,000	700	1,000	3,000
Stocks	48,817	35,121	37,079	39,329	42,596
Disappearance					
Europe	460	545	412	700	500
Americas	4,541	4,913	2,919	3,100	4,200
Other	2,181	3,694	5,980	4,900	3,900
Total Exports	7,182	9,152	9,311	8,700	8,600
Domestic	33,694	23,139	24,765	25,209	27,414
Seed, Feed, Waste	1,940	2,129	2,002	2,420	2,582
Total Usage	42,817	34,421	36,078	36,329	38,596
Ending Stocks	6,000	700	1,000	3,000	4,000
Stocks/Use Ratio	14.0 %	2.0 %	2.8 %	8.3 %	10.4 %

Forecasts by STAT Market Research based on data from the USDA and U.S. Department of Commerce

Canadian Kidney & Navy Bean Exports April, 2014

(metric tons)

Crop Year	2011-12	2012-13	2012-13	2013-14	2014
Period	Aug-Jul	Aug-Jul	Aug-Apr	Aug-Apr	Apr
Top Five Buyers					
United Kingdom	47,972	54,565	42,297	39,590	3,185
Italy	10,987	17,705	13,369	14,480	1,627
Turkey	68	3,867	3,071	9,824	500
United States	21,309	15,774	11,677	9,620	1,455
Algeria	0	375	250	5,570	0
Subtotal	80,336	92,286	70,663	79,083	6,768
Percent of Total	77.1%	73.7%	73.4%	70.2%	61.8%
All Buyers					
Saint Pierre and Miquelon	0	1	0	0	0
United States	21,309	15,774	11,677	9,620	1,455
Total N. America	21,309	15,775	11,677	9,620	1,455

Canadian Kidney & Navy Bean Exports April, 2014 Con't
(metric tons)

Crop Year Period	2011-12 Aug-Jul	2012-13 Aug-Jul	2012-13 Aug-Apr	2013-14 Aug-Apr	2014 Apr
Belgium	147	179	139	813	345
France	585	931	806	989	112
Germany	3,936	3,249	2,225	2,493	298
Greece	1,412	107	107	40	0
Ireland	1,522	1,688	1,438	1,479	125
Italy	10,987	17,705	13,369	14,480	1,627
Malta	0	61	20	91	20
Netherlands	990	4,045	3,903	1,648	0
Portugal	294	611	611	1,148	0
Spain	832	991	789	1,560	98
Switzerland	0	0	0	244	0
United Kingdom	47,972	54,565	42,297	39,590	3,185
Total W. Europe	68,676	84,132	65,704	64,574	5,811
Albania	0	20	20	40	0
Bosnia and Herzegovina	180	140	140	367	0
Bulgaria	0	25	25	2,348	200
Croatia	454	434	354	318	78
Czech Republic	25	25	25	0	0
Hungary	0	74	74	165	0
Palestine	0	121	121	0	0
Romania	0	0	0	841	600
Russia	0	21	21	360	0
Serbia	160	20	20	600	60
Slovenia	691	108	41	199	0
Turkmenistan	0	0	0	224	0
Ukraine	0	20	20	197	0
Total E. Europe	1,510	1,007	860	5,659	938
Egypt	0	0	0	125	0
Israel	0	0	0	693	100
Jordan	0	25	0	24	0
Kuwait	0	7	2	0	0
Lebanon	0	52	40	52	12
Saudi Arabia	0	10	10	1,320	82
Turkey	68	3,867	3,071	9,824	500
United Arab Emirates	24	188	188	1,653	175
Total Middle East	92	4,149	3,311	13,691	869

Canadian Kidney & Navy Bean Exports April, 2014 Con't
(metric tons)

Crop Year	2011-12	2012-13	2012-13	2013-14	2014
Period	Aug-Jul	Aug-Jul	Aug-Apr	Aug-Apr	Apr
Algeria	0	375	250	5,570	0
Angola	286	2,001	1,906	725	0
Burkina Faso	2	1	1	0	0
Cape Verde	0	21	0	0	0
Equatorial Guinea	0	6	0	0	0
Mauritius	0	0	0	41	0
South Africa	0	818	419	474	239
Swaziland	0	0	0	20	0
Total Africa	287	3,221	2,575	6,830	239
China	0	21	0	1,910	575
Hong Kong	40	1	1	0	0
India	0	0	0	670	0
Japan	1,334	1,337	1,199	747	0
Korea North	40	0	0	0	0
Korea South	3,765	4,621	3,516	3,547	586
Malaysia	23	40	40	63	0
Singapore	0	1	1	0	0
Total Asia	5,201	6,021	4,757	6,937	1,161
Australia	2,043	1,919	1,407	816	230
New Zealand	874	1,137	505	591	110
U.S. Minor Outlying Islands	68	0	0	0	0
Total Pacific	2,985	3,056	1,912	1,408	340
Argentina	0	0	0	25	0
Brazil	0	0	0	125	0
Chile	0	695	495	434	50
Colombia	270	1,461	1,087	747	0
Guyana	2	1	1	1	0
Peru	0	561	361	153	0
Venezuela	841	618	298	699	0
Total S. America	1,112	3,336	2,242	2,184	50

Canadian Kidney & Navy Bean Exports April, 2014

(metric tons)

Crop Year Period	2011-12 Aug-Jul	2012-13 Aug-Jul	2012-13 Aug-Apr	2013-14 Aug-Apr	2014 Apr
Antigua and Barbuda	6	45	35	20	6
Aruba	3	2	2	2	0
Barbados	1	0	0	1	0
Costa Rica	0	150	0	223	25
Cuba	0	21	18	0	0
Dominica	54	37	25	60	4
Dominican Republic	610	402	402	449	0
Grenada	14	14	13	10	0
Jamaica	468	291	209	230	20
Mexico	1,491	3,151	2,087	182	0
Panama	56	182	182	397	0
Saint Lucia	9	2	1	1	0
Saint Vincent and the Grenadines	2	1	0	0	0
Trinidad	252	266	238	141	25
Turks and Caicos Islands	0	1	1	1	0
Total C. America	2,965	4,563	3,215	1,716	81
Total World	104,138	125,261	96,253	112,618	10,944

Source: Statistics Canada

U.S. Dark Red Kidney Bean Exports April, 2014

(metric tons)

Crop Year	2011-12	2012-13	2012-13	2013-14	2014
Period	Sep-Aug	Sep-Aug	Sep-Apr	Sep-Apr	Apr
Top Five Buyers					
Italy	2,931	7,690	4,740	6,983	0
United Kingdom	135	2,320	1,318	4,546	50
France	1,588	3,058	2,771	4,105	513
Canada	1,263	1,132	967	3,648	1,025
Russia	1,498	2,284	1,950	1,477	0
Subtotal	7,415	16,483	11,746	20,759	1,589
Percent of Total	43.7%	60.4%	56.9%	72.0%	68.9%
All Buyers					
Canada	1,263	1,132	967	3,648	1,025
Total N. America	1,263	1,132	967	3,648	1,025
Austria	0	45	45	65	0
Belgium	1,307	2,646	2,302	1,372	76
Denmark	167	116	116	116	0
France	1,588	3,058	2,771	4,105	513
Germany	145	567	327	1,135	54
Greece	54	33	33	49	0
Italy	2,931	7,690	4,740	6,983	0
Netherlands	302	0	0	286	0
Portugal	0	0	0	888	0
Spain	19	707	388	655	0
Switzerland	0	187	131	249	139
United Kingdom	135	2,320	1,318	4,546	50
Total W. Europe	6,648	17,367	12,169	20,448	831
Hungary	0	502	502	777	209
Poland	0	1,135	1,135	753	98
Russia	1,498	2,284	1,950	1,477	0
Total E. Europe	1,498	3,921	3,587	3,008	306
Saudi Arabia	0	0	0	42	0
Turkey	88	74	74	0	0
United Arab Emirates	0	0	0	467	0
Total Middle East	88	74	74	509	0
Nigeria	0	15	15	0	0
Total Africa	0	15	15	0	0

U.S. Dark Red Kidney Bean Exports April, 2014

(metric tons)

Crop Year Period	2011-12 Sep-Aug	2012-13 Sep-Aug	2012-13 Sep-Apr	2013-14 Sep-Apr	2014 Apr
China	0	20	20	0	0
Hong Kong	26	58	58	0	0
India	18	0	0	0	0
Japan	1,656	1,296	628	390	22
Korea South	61	458	458	159	0
Malaysia	0	45	0	0	0
Taiwan	0	0	0	23	0
Total Asia	1,761	1,877	1,164	571	22
Australia	95	391	267	173	120
New Zealand	22	0	0	69	0
Total Pacific	117	391	267	242	120
Colombia	0	184	184	4	0
Total S. America	0	184	184	4	0
Costa Rica	0	12	12	0	0
Dominican Republic	3,302	370	370	0	0
Guatemala	572	945	904	0	0
Honduras	7	17	17	0	0
Jamaica	21	190	190	0	0
Leeward Windward Is.	19	21	20	11	0
Mexico	1,197	306	306	181	0
Netherlands Antilles	10	22	10	2	0
Nicaragua	473	398	398	189	0
Trinidad	0	49	0	0	0
Total C. America	5,600	2,330	2,227	384	0
Total World	16,975	27,290	20,654	28,813	2,305

Source: U.S. Department of Commerce

U.S. Light Red Kidney Bean Exports April, 2014

(metric tons)

Crop Year	2011-12	2012-13	2012-13	2013-14	2014
Period	Sep-Aug	Sep-Aug	Sep-Apr	Sep-Apr	Apr
Top Five Buyers					
Canada	990	1,057	786	1,223	57
France	1,918	833	470	602	8
United Arab Emirates	0	0	0	586	0
Panama	45	160	0	180	0
Trinidad	41	112	75	171	0
Subtotal	2,995	2,162	1,331	2,760	65
Percent of Total	52.5%	63.2%	61.5%	81.0%	50.7%
All Buyers					
Canada	990	1,057	786	1,223	57
Total N. America	990	1,057	786	1,223	57
Belgium	0	20	0	18	0
France	1,918	833	470	602	8
Germany	0	6	6	0	0
Italy	5	0	0	0	0
Netherlands	436	112	75	83	17
Norway	73	0	0	0	0
Portugal	0	173	0	112	0
United Kingdom	28	0	0	20	0
Total W. Europe	2,460	1,145	551	834	24
Slovakia	0	0	0	4	0
Total E. Europe	0	0	0	4	0
United Arab Emirates	0	0	0	586	0
Total Middle East	0	0	0	586	0
Liberia	0	0	0	98	38
Total Africa	0	0	0	98	38
China	0	0	0	4	0
Hong Kong	2	11	11	10	0
India	18	71	0	0	0
Korea South	16	20	0	0	0
Philippines	0	3	3	3	0
Taiwan	82	0	0	21	0
Total Asia	118	104	13	39	0
Australia	88	8	8	60	0
New Zealand	0	0	0	4	0
Total Pacific	88	8	8	64	0

U.S. Light Red Kidney Bean Exports April, 2014
(metric tons)

Crop Year	2011-12	2012-13	2012-13	2013-14	2014
Period	Sep-Aug	Sep-Aug	Sep-Apr	Sep-Apr	Apr
Argentina	21	0	0	0	0
Colombia	5	246	216	0	0
French Guiana	0	0	0	10	0
Guyana	4	9	9	0	0
Suriname	5	4	1	1	0
Total S. America	34	259	226	11	0
Barbados	11	9	7	10	0
Belize	0	0	0	23	0
Bermuda	7	6	4	11	0
Cayman Islands	0	0	0	1	0
Costa Rica	0	42	21	41	0
Dominican Republic	3	112	90	1	1
Guatemala	2	1	1	19	0
Jamaica	1,313	164	162	54	0
Leeward Windward Is.	16	33	25	18	0
Mexico	485	166	166	0	0
Netherlands Antilles	91	46	32	24	7
Panama	45	160	0	180	0
Trinidad	41	112	75	171	0
Total C. America	2,012	849	582	551	8
Total World	5,702	3,423	2,165	3,409	128

Source: U.S. Department of Commerce

U.S. Kidney (nes) Bean Exports April, 2014

(metric tons)

Crop Year	2011-12	2012-13	2012-13	2013-14	2014
Period	Sep-Aug	Sep-Aug	Sep-Apr	Sep-Apr	Apr
Top Five Buyers					
Netherlands	3,154	3,137	2,955	4,545	348
Canada	7,173	10,884	7,188	4,391	1,909
Mexico	18,123	28,665	20,954	4,124	861
Hungary	0	1,663	1,576	3,960	51
France	675	1,126	1,026	1,602	0
Subtotal	29,124	45,474	33,697	18,622	3,169
Percent of Total	78.2%	84.0%	85.7%	73.7%	86.7%
All Buyers					
Canada	7,173	10,884	7,188	4,391	1,909
Total N. America	7,173	10,884	7,188	4,391	1,909
Belgium	0	140	60	704	0
France	675	1,126	1,026	1,602	0
Germany	3,099	1,271	1,151	126	0
Greece	0	56	56	0	0
Italy	0	74	74	169	0
Netherlands	3,154	3,137	2,955	4,545	348
Portugal	0	165	0	80	0
Spain	20	0	0	514	0
Switzerland	0	160	80	80	0
United Kingdom	3	0	0	20	0
Total W. Europe	6,950	6,128	5,401	7,841	348
Hungary	0	1,663	1,576	3,960	51
Russia	0	0	0	163	0
Total E. Europe	0	1,663	1,576	4,123	51
Cyprus	7	0	0	0	0
Iran	25	0	0	0	0
Iraq	0	0	0	1	0
Israel	219	232	232	305	0
Jordan	144	47	34	126	57
Lebanon	19	212	149	49	0
Oman	38	0	0	0	0
Qatar	0	1	0	0	0
Saudi Arabia	214	494	354	317	0
Syria	5	10	10	1	0
Turkey	681	193	193	20	0
United Arab Emirates	2	1	1	23	1
Total Middle East	1,354	1,189	973	842	57

U.S. Kidney (nes) Bean Exports April, 2014

(metric tons)

Crop Year	2011-12	2012-13	2012-13	2013-14	2014
Period	Sep-Aug	Sep-Aug	Sep-Apr	Sep-Apr	Apr
Algeria	0	0	0	112	0
Djibouti	0	0	0	2	2
Kenya	200	425	264	0	0
Liberia	121	99	60	38	0
Mauritius	2	1	1	1	0
Mayotte	0	189	0	0	0
Morocco	0	31	19	165	0
South Africa	376	473	350	349	0
Tanzania	19	18	18	10	0
Total Africa	717	1,236	711	677	2
China	0	0	0	13	0
Hong Kong	73	136	113	142	50
India	321	609	161	347	71
Japan	289	191	87	233	61
Korea South	0	2	0	0	0
Pakistan	60	113	40	41	0
Philippines	2	0	0	0	0
Singapore	40	0	0	0	0
Sri Lanka	21	0	0	0	0
Thailand	104	210	186	221	0
Total Asia	909	1,261	586	996	182
Australia	1,046	1,457	1,117	1,246	96
New Zealand	77	194	120	73	18
South Georgia and the South Sandwich Islands	0	8	8	0	0
Total Pacific	1,123	1,659	1,244	1,320	113
Argentina	1	36	3	84	13
Brazil	239	183	98	133	56
Chile	153	120	56	360	20
Colombia	10	19	0	9	0
French Guiana	19	0	0	0	0
Peru	22	2	2	0	0
Suriname	48	0	0	0	0
Uruguay	0	1	0	0	0
Venezuela	94	42	0	0	0

U.S. Kidney (nes) Bean Exports April, 2014
(metric tons)

Crop Year	2011-12	2012-13	2012-13	2013-14	2014
Period	Sep-Aug	Sep-Aug	Sep-Apr	Sep-Apr	Apr
Total S. America	586	403	158	585	89
Bahamas	0	0	0	12	0
Barbados	12	0	0	0	0
Belize	0	0	0	135	0
Cayman Islands	0	0	0	1	0
Costa Rica	53	21	21	20	0
Dominican Republic	15	394	394	0	0
El Salvador	1	0	0	1	0
Guatemala	115	448	29	48	0
Honduras	0	19	18	0	0
Jamaica	36	40	1	0	0
Leeward Windward Is.	21	0	0	0	0
Mexico	18,123	28,665	20,954	4,124	861
Netherlands Antilles	20	0	0	0	0
Nicaragua	33	0	0	0	0
Panama	0	62	62	122	43
Trinidad	0	38	2	23	1
Total C. America	18,430	29,687	21,481	4,486	905
Total World	37,242	54,109	39,317	25,261	3,656

Source: U.S. Department of Commerce

Pinto Beans

U.S. Pinto Bean Supply and Demand Estimates
(metric tons, acres)

Year	2010	2011	2012	2013	2014
Acreage	842,700	386,700	729,700	485,100	668,400
Yield (lbs)	1,639	1,519	1,855	1,749	1,670
Production	626,599	266,443	613,898	384,922	506,187
Carryin	25,000	170,000	3,900	86,000	37,000
Stocks	651,599	436,443	617,798	470,923	543,187
Disappearance					
Europe	1,790	340	2,952	4,000	2,000
Americas	58,013	154,202	91,130	51,000	86,000
Other	22,289	8,614	21,427	21,000	21,000
Total Exports	82,092	163,156	115,509	76,000	109,000
Domestic	385,377	242,939	398,596	333,171	359,804
Seed, Feed, Waste	14,130	26,448	17,693	24,752	25,383
Total Usage	481,599	432,543	531,798	433,923	494,187
Ending Stocks	170,000	3,900	86,000	37,000	49,000
Stocks/Use Ratio	35.3 %	0.9 %	16.2 %	8.5 %	9.9 %

Forecasts by STAT Market Research based on data from the USDA and U.S. Department of Commerce

U.S. Pinto Bean Exports April, 2014
(metric tons)

Crop Year	2011-12	2012-13	2012-13	2013-14	2014
Period	Sep-Aug	Sep-Aug	Sep-Apr	Sep-Apr	Apr
Top Five Buyers					
Dominican Republic	18,404	27,977	21,552	14,555	1,830
Angola	1,270	9,748	6,057	7,025	117
Mexico	102,611	42,997	25,839	5,645	1,071
Algeria	0	0	0	4,617	0
Haiti	1,123	5,987	4,772	2,608	181
Subtotal	123,408	86,709	58,220	34,450	3,199
Percent of Total	92.6%	83.5%	80.7%	78.9%	76.2%

U.S. Pinto Bean Exports April, 2014

(metric tons)

Crop Year	2011-12	2012-13	2012-13	2013-14	2014
Period	Sep-Aug	Sep-Aug	Sep-Apr	Sep-Apr	Apr
All Buyers					
Belgium	0	425	384	438	21
Denmark	36	0	0	0	0
Germany	0	86	86	0	0
Italy	0	250	187	354	0
Netherlands	95	991	864	239	2
Norway	0	2	2	0	0
Portugal	0	287	162	146	63
Spain	45	147	63	734	25
United Kingdom	59	0	0	2	2
Total W. Europe	235	2,188	1,748	1,913	112
Bulgaria	0	20	20	42	0
Croatia	0	63	0	0	0
Hungary	0	386	200	292	21
Russia	0	142	142	0	0
Slovenia	60	0	0	0	0
Yugoslavia	0	21	0	125	0
Total E. Europe	60	631	361	459	21
Ethiopia	320	0	0	0	0
Kuwait	18	0	0	0	0
Saudi Arabia	3	0	0	0	0
Turkey	44	154	22	563	408
United Arab Emirates	5	0	0	246	0
Yemen	1,884	0	0	0	0
Total Middle East	2,275	154	22	809	408
Algeria	0	0	0	4,617	0
Angola	1,270	9,748	6,057	7,025	117
Cameroon	0	650	300	269	35
Congo	890	789	789	0	0
Cote D'ivoire	1,520	0	0	0	0
Ghana	0	0	0	2	0
Kenya	0	1,122	1,122	0	0
Liberia	0	0	0	42	42
Malawi	948	190	0	0	0
Mozambique	0	3,642	3,642	0	0
Tanzania	0	3,458	3,458	882	180
Total Africa	4,628	19,598	15,367	12,837	374

U.S. Pinto Bean Exports April, 2014
(metric tons)

Crop Year	2011-12	2012-13	2012-13	2013-14	2014
Period	Sep-Aug	Sep-Aug	Sep-Apr	Sep-Apr	Apr
India	0	1,134	666	1,923	46
Japan	11	6	6	21	21
Philippines	0	4	4	4	0
Thailand	2	0	0	0	0
Total Asia	13	1,143	676	1,948	67
Australia	297	229	168	123	0
New Zealand	25	21	21	27	0
Total Pacific	323	250	188	150	0
Argentina	5	0	0	0	0
Chile	0	180	180	689	136
Colombia	1	1,062	0	0	0
Ecuador	240	0	0	0	0
Peru	0	45	45	0	0
Suriname	1	2	2	0	0
Total S. America	248	1,289	227	689	136
Bermuda	0	0	0	4	0
Costa Rica	19	0	0	0	0
Dominican Republic	18,404	27,977	21,552	14,555	1,830
El Salvador	1	0	0	0	0
Guatemala	1,939	1,131	991	1,149	0
Haiti	1,123	5,987	4,772	2,608	181
Jamaica	1	0	0	0	0
Mexico	102,611	42,997	25,839	5,645	1,071
Netherlands Antilles	4	14	10	5	0
Nicaragua	0	0	0	80	0
Panama	3	21	0	0	0
Trinidad	22	5	5	0	0
Total C. America	124,128	78,131	53,169	24,046	3,082
Other	1,420	410	389	829	0
Total	1,420	410	389	829	0
Total World	133,330	103,794	72,146	43,679	4,200

Source: U.S. Department of Commerce

Canadian Pinto Bean Exports April, 2014

(metric tons)

Crop Year	2011-12	2012-13	2012-13	2013-14	2014
Period	Aug-Jul	Aug-Jul	Aug-Apr	Aug-Apr	Apr
Top Five Buyers					
Angola	7,756	29,055	23,861	16,866	3,706
United States	2,700	2,386	1,959	3,017	404
Italy	283	1,510	1,388	1,959	50
Mexico	10,628	8,290	6,629	1,699	139
Portugal	468	4,754	4,629	1,446	25
Subtotal	21,835	45,996	38,467	24,987	4,324
Percent of Total	85.7%	78.1%	79.9%	77.4%	82.9%
All Buyers					
United States	2,700	2,386	1,959	3,017	404
Total N. America	2,700	2,386	1,959	3,017	404
Belgium	53	124	99	25	0
France	104	195	195	68	24
Germany	0	466	441	572	75
Italy	283	1,510	1,388	1,959	50
Netherlands	1	795	795	1	0
Portugal	468	4,754	4,629	1,446	25
Spain	667	499	399	297	0
Switzerland	0	150	100	100	0
United Kingdom	801	1,065	591	723	44
Total W. Europe	2,378	9,557	8,637	5,191	217
Albania	0	0	0	25	25
Bulgaria	0	342	292	682	133
Croatia	20	0	0	190	0
Czech Republic	25	215	45	264	0
Georgia	0	0	0	75	0
Hungary	0	290	141	245	23
Slovakia	0	50	0	25	0
Slovenia	0	21	21	0	0
Yugoslavia	0	50	0	0	0
Total E. Europe	45	968	499	1,506	181
Cyprus	0	125	0	0	0
Israel	0	0	0	25	25
Saudi Arabia	0	0	0	82	0
Turkey	0	216	216	250	0
United Arab Emirates	0	0	0	374	299
Total Middle East	0	340	216	731	324

Canadian Pinto Bean Exports April, 2014

(metric tons)

Crop Year	2011-12	2012-13	2012-13	2013-14	2014
Period	Aug-Jul	Aug-Jul	Aug-Apr	Aug-Apr	Apr
Algeria	0	49	49	500	0
Angola	7,756	29,055	23,861	16,866	3,706
Cape Verde	0	197	73	174	25
Comoros	141	0	0	0	0
Congo	0	50	0	274	0
Congo Democratic Republic (Zaire)	0	249	249	0	0
Liberia	0	0	0	25	0
South Africa	0	222	222	150	0
Total Africa	7,896	29,823	24,455	17,989	3,731
China	0	74	74	0	0
India	0	0	0	444	0
Total Asia	0	74	74	444	0
Australia	86	472	285	81	22
New Zealand	10	10	10	0	0
U.S. Minor Outlying Islands	268	200	200	25	0
Total Pacific	363	682	495	106	22
Brazil	150	0	0	0	0
Chile	472	3,365	2,425	798	199
Uruguay	0	22	0	0	0
Total S. America	622	3,387	2,425	798	199
Dominican Republic	657	3,125	2,754	793	0
Haiti	181	249	0	0	0
Jamaica	1	0	0	0	0
Mexico	10,628	8,290	6,629	1,699	139
Panama	8	9	9	16	0
Trinidad	3	18	14	11	0
Total C. America	11,479	11,692	9,405	2,519	139
Total World	25,483	58,909	48,165	32,300	5,217

Source: Statistics Canada

White Beans

U.S. Navy and Pea Bean Supply and Demand Estimates
(metric tons, acres)

Year	2010	2011	2012	2013	2014
Acreage	279,500	204,400	262,800	174,200	262,700
Yield (lbs)	1,705	1,589	1,867	1,953	1,768
Production	216,184	147,328	222,535	154,314	210,704
Carryin	10,000	30,000	3,000	20,000	1,000
Stocks	226,184	177,328	225,535	174,314	211,704
Disappearance					
Europe	52,557	51,426	40,705	61,000	54,000
Americas	27,768	39,175	52,424	70,000	45,000
Other	7,523	9,528	12,451	16,000	10,000
Total Exports	87,849	100,128	105,581	147,000	109,000
Domestic	104,164	68,835	96,398	22,874	86,295
Seed, Feed, Waste	4,172	5,364	3,556	3,440	5,409
Total Usage	196,185	174,328	205,534	173,314	200,704
Ending Stocks	30,000	3,000	20,000	1,000	11,000
Stocks/Use Ratio	15.3 %	1.7 %	9.7 %	0.6 %	5.5 %

Forecasts by STAT Market Research based on data from the USDA and U.S. Department of Commerce

U.S. Pea Bean Exports April, 2014
(metric tons)

Crop Year	2011-12	2012-13	2012-13	2013-14	2014
Period	Sep-Aug	Sep-Aug	Sep-Apr	Sep-Apr	Apr
Top Five Buyers					
Canada	31,789	42,083	24,285	41,057	3,106
United Kingdom	38,109	30,333	18,571	28,691	2,807
Mexico	11,550	19,260	9,981	25,653	1,972
Turkey	0	0	0	12,441	4,034
Italy	12,675	9,275	7,214	9,287	1,094
Subtotal	94,123	100,950	60,051	117,128	13,012
Percent of Total	90.2%	87.2%	84.3%	81.6%	73.8%
All Buyers					
Canada	31,789	42,083	24,285	41,057	3,106
Total N. America	31,789	42,083	24,285	41,057	3,106
Belgium	0	21	21	1,768	0
France	0	48	21	0	0
Germany	128	85	85	39	0
Italy	12,675	9,275	7,214	9,287	1,094
Netherlands	0	0	0	2,817	1,123
Portugal	0	0	0	426	0
Spain	554	751	581	1,397	149
United Kingdom	38,109	30,333	18,571	28,691	2,807
Total W. Europe	51,467	40,513	26,493	44,425	5,173
Bulgaria	0	0	0	1,268	0
Poland	0	0	0	296	296
Russia	0	218	218	804	0
Total E. Europe	0	218	218	2,367	296
Israel	0	0	0	59	20
Saudi Arabia	0	0	0	1,309	1,309
Syria	0	0	0	1	1
Turkey	0	0	0	12,441	4,034
Yemen	521	0	0	0	0
Total Middle East	521	0	0	13,808	5,363
Malawi	0	1,198	1,198	0	0
South Africa	0	1,521	1,521	7,283	0
Total Africa	0	2,720	2,720	7,283	0
Japan	206	223	184	142	61
Korea South	294	622	267	380	0
Thailand	5	0	0	0	0
Total Asia	505	845	451	522	61
New Zealand	8,513	8,967	6,176	6,734	1,431
Total Pacific	8,513	8,967	6,176	6,734	1,431

U.S. Pea Bean Exports April, 2014

(metric tons)

Crop Year	2011-12	2012-13	2012-13	2013-14	2014
Period	Sep-Aug	Sep-Aug	Sep-Apr	Sep-Apr	Apr
Argentina	2	0	0	0	0
Brazil	5	0	0	0	0
Chile	0	0	0	147	20
Colombia	0	598	462	450	0
French Guiana	0	0	0	22	0
Peru	0	462	417	43	0
Total S. America	7	1,060	879	662	20
Costa Rica	0	61	10	497	76
Dominican Republic	0	0	0	333	0
Jamaica	20	43	21	21	0
Mexico	11,550	19,260	9,981	25,653	1,972
Panama	4	3	3	3	0
Trinidad	7	6	6	204	136
Total C. America	11,581	19,372	10,021	26,710	2,183
Total World	104,382	115,777	71,242	143,568	17,632

Source: U.S. Department of Commerce

Canadian Navy or Pea Bean Exports April, 2014

(metric tons)

Crop Year	2011-12	2012-13	2012-13	2013-14	2014
Period	Aug-Jul	Aug-Jul	Aug-Apr	Aug-Apr	Apr
Top Five Buyers					
United Kingdom	45,130	52,200	40,091	38,492	3,105
Italy	9,242	16,800	12,570	13,443	1,607
Turkey	0	3,867	3,071	9,475	500
Algeria	0	375	250	5,329	0
Korea South	3,553	4,283	3,391	3,154	586
Subtotal	57,925	77,524	59,373	69,893	5,799
Percent of Total	76.7%	73.8%	73.4%	73.9%	61.3%
All Buyers					
United States	7,457	5,124	4,469	2,472	595
Total N. America	7,457	5,124	4,469	2,472	595

Canadian Navy or Pea Bean Exports April, 2014
(metric tons)

Crop Year	2011-12	2012-13	2012-13	2013-14	2014
Period	Aug-Jul	Aug-Jul	Aug-Apr	Aug-Apr	Apr
Belgium	83	179	139	773	345
France	310	476	412	703	108
Germany	2,082	3,150	2,126	2,417	276
Greece	2	0	0	0	0
Ireland	1,502	1,648	1,398	1,439	125
Italy	9,242	16,800	12,570	13,443	1,607
Malta	0	61	20	41	20
Netherlands	846	3,979	3,838	1,411	0
Portugal	74	248	248	823	0
Spain	546	689	487	1,121	98
Switzerland	0	0	0	244	0
United Kingdom	45,130	52,200	40,091	38,492	3,105
Total W. Europe	59,817	79,430	61,329	60,907	5,685
Bulgaria	0	25	25	1,974	200
Croatia	0	71	71	0	0
Czech Republic	25	25	25	0	0
Hungary	0	74	74	125	0
Romania	0	0	0	741	600
Russia	0	21	21	360	0
Turkmenistan	0	0	0	224	0
Ukraine	0	0	0	197	0
Yugoslavia	0	21	21	0	0
Total E. Europe	25	237	237	3,620	800
Egypt	0	0	0	125	0
Israel	0	0	0	618	100
Jordan	0	25	0	24	0
Saudi Arabia	0	0	0	1,195	82
Turkey	0	3,867	3,071	9,475	500
United Arab Emirates	0	188	188	799	175
Total Middle East	0	4,080	3,259	12,235	856
Algeria	0	375	250	5,329	0
Angola	0	1,801	1,706	725	0
Mauritius	0	0	0	41	0
South Africa	0	717	419	474	239
Total Africa	0	2,893	2,374	6,569	239

Canadian Navy or Pea Bean Exports April, 2014

(metric tons)

Crop Year	2011-12	2012-13	2012-13	2013-14	2014
Period	Aug-Jul	Aug-Jul	Aug-Apr	Aug-Apr	Apr
China	0	21	0	1,623	363
Hong Kong	40	0	0	0	0
India	0	0	0	670	0
Japan	0	286	286	21	0
Korea North	40	0	0	0	0
Korea South	3,553	4,283	3,391	3,154	586
Malaysia	0	40	40	40	0
Total Asia	3,633	4,630	3,717	5,509	949
Australia	1,598	1,418	1,000	574	205
New Zealand	770	1,015	429	390	20
Total Pacific	2,369	2,432	1,430	964	224
Argentina	0	0	0	25	0
Brazil	0	0	0	125	0
Chile	0	695	495	299	50
Colombia	150	1,153	779	747	0
Peru	0	561	361	100	0
Total S. America	150	2,409	1,635	1,296	50
Antigua and Barbuda	6	45	35	20	6
Aruba	3	2	2	2	0
Costa Rica	0	150	0	198	25
Cuba	0	10	10	0	0
Dominica	54	37	25	60	4
Dominican Republic	386	103	103	249	0
Grenada	14	13	12	8	0
Jamaica	313	290	209	230	20
Mexico	1,205	2,989	1,925	182	0
Panama	0	29	29	25	0
Saint Lucia	3	1	1	1	0
Saint Vincent and the Grenadines	1	0	0	0	0
Trinidad	125	111	107	66	0
Turks and Caicos Islands	0	1	1	1	0
Total C. America	2,110	3,782	2,459	1,042	55
Total World	75,560	105,016	80,909	94,613	9,455

Source: Statistics Canada

Fababeans

Canadian Fababean Exports April, 2014
(metric tons)

Crop Year	2011-12	2012-13	2012-13	2013-14	2014
Period	Aug-Jul	Aug-Jul	Aug-Apr	Aug-Apr	Apr
Egypt	894	1,426	1,121	6,657	1,233
Haiti	0	1	1	0	0
Israel	0	0	0	108	0
Italy	80	0	0	0	0
Jordan	50	0	0	0	0
Kuwait	0	24	4	0	0
Lebanon	46	124	124	125	0
United States	1,374	899	779	1,124	59
Total World	2,444	2,473	2,029	8,013	1,292

Source: Statistics Canada

Australian Broadbean (faba) Exports April, 2014

(metric tons)

Crop Year	2011-12	2012-13	2012-13	2013-14	2014
Period	Nov-Oct	Nov-Oct	Nov-Apr	Nov-Apr	Apr
Top Five Buyers					
Egypt	194,747	202,577	167,496	210,945	6,564
Saudi Arabia	38,291	35,357	27,307	42,563	6,628
United Arab Emirates	15,016	14,254	6,516	10,712	2,282
Indonesia	10,056	11,358	5,051	9,847	2,979
Lebanon	1,839	5,708	3,410	4,890	911
Subtotal	259,949	269,254	209,781	278,958	19,363
Percent of Total	88.6%	88.8%	90.0%	95.6%	89.3%
All Buyers					
Canada	0	0	0	107	22
United States	200	204	150	0	0
Total N. America	200	204	150	107	22
Belgium	39	58	20	38	0
Italy	822	863	259	282	0
Malta	0	23	23	23	0
Portugal	0	16	0	0	0
Spain	952	364	161	610	95
United Kingdom	23	23	0	23	0
Total W. Europe	1,836	1,347	463	976	95
Bahrain	79	122	122	139	19
Cyprus	22	0	0	0	0
Egypt	194,747	202,577	167,496	210,945	6,564
Israel	360	585	301	237	0
Jordan	4,224	6,685	3,984	2,901	636
Kuwait	506	616	528	560	88
Lebanon	1,839	5,708	3,410	4,890	911
Qatar	46	23	23	18	0
Saudi Arabia	38,291	35,357	27,307	42,563	6,628
Sudan	8,000	6,300	6,300	0	0
Turkey	510	69	0	629	123
United Arab Emirates	15,016	14,254	6,516	10,712	2,282
Yemen	6,215	8,570	6,650	2,498	161
Total Middle East	269,855	280,867	222,637	276,091	17,412
Algeria	108	0	0	0	0
Kenya	44	0	0	0	0
Mauritius	0	72	48	0	0
South Africa	150	93	0	0	0
Total Africa	302	165	48	0	0

Australian Broadbean (faba) Exports April, 2014

(metric tons)

Crop Year	2011-12	2012-13	2012-13	2013-14	2014
Period	Nov-Oct	Nov-Oct	Nov-Apr	Nov-Apr	Apr
Bangladesh	0	480	0	0	0
Hong Kong	0	1	0	0	0
India	22	72	0	0	0
Indonesia	10,056	11,358	5,051	9,847	2,979
Japan	1,014	837	278	321	64
Malaysia	5,241	2,361	1,157	796	322
Pakistan	217	257	107	149	0
Philippines	951	928	409	585	67
Singapore	104	66	0	0	0
Sri Lanka	72	144	120	0	0
Taiwan	1,862	2,619	1,552	1,408	341
Thailand	1,209	1,250	700	546	130
Vietnam	0	0	0	174	109
Total Asia	20,746	20,373	9,375	13,827	4,012
Mexico	600	387	301	913	149
Total C. America	600	387	301	913	149
Total World	293,539	303,343	232,973	291,914	21,689

Source: Australia Bureau of Statistics

Canadian Fababean Exports April, 2014

(metric tons)

Crop Year	2011-12	2012-13	2012-13	2013-14	2014
Period	Aug-Jul	Aug-Jul	Aug-Apr	Aug-Apr	Apr
Egypt	894	1,426	1,121	6,657	1,233
Haiti	0	1	1	0	0
Israel	0	0	0	108	0
Italy	80	0	0	0	0
Jordan	50	0	0	0	0
Kuwait	0	24	4	0	0
Lebanon	46	124	124	125	0
United States	1,374	899	779	1,124	59
Total World	2,444	2,473	2,029	8,013	1,292

Source: Statistics Canada

U.S. Broadbean Exports April, 2014
(metric tons)

Crop Year	2011-12	2012-13	2012-13	2013-14	2014
Period	Sep-Aug	Sep-Aug	Sep-Apr	Sep-Apr	Apr
Top Five Buyers					
Canada	51	4,823	1,648	9,140	1,429
Subtotal	51	4,823	1,648	9,140	1,429
Percent of Total	9.5%	96.5%	95.8%	99.8%	100.0%
All Buyers					
Canada	51	4,823	1,648	9,140	1,429
Total N. America	51	4,823	1,648	9,140	1,429
Italy	0	36	36	0	0
Netherlands	0	22	22	0	0
Sweden	0	0	0	10	0
United Kingdom	3	0	0	0	0
Total W. Europe	3	58	58	10	0
Egypt	0	83	0	0	0
Israel	8	0	0	0	0
Jordan	37	0	0	0	0
Total Middle East	45	83	0	0	0
Algeria	419	0	0	0	0
Total Africa	419	0	0	0	0
Japan	0	20	0	0	0
Total Asia	0	20	0	0	0
Peru	0	0	0	5	0
Total S. America	0	0	0	5	0
Dominican Republic	17	0	0	0	0
Guatemala	0	14	14	0	0
Mexico	0	1	0	0	0
Total C. America	17	15	14	0	0
Total World	535	4,998	1,721	9,155	1,429

Source: U.S. Department of Commerce

Black Beans

U.S. Black Bean Supply and Demand Estimates
(metric tons, acres)

Year	2010	2011	2012	2013	2014
Acreage	284,000	183,900	216,800	143,100	141,700
Yield (lbs)	1,641	1,641	1,725	1,778	1,735
Production	211,422	136,896	169,600	115,440	111,504
Carryin	1,000	43,000	50,000	75,000	62,000
Stocks	212,422	179,896	219,600	190,440	173,504
Disappearance					
Europe	1,012	644	468	800	700
Americas	105,046	64,345	54,196	36,400	68,500
Other	1,268	1,848	1,200	1,800	1,300
Total Exports	115,069	66,837	55,864	39,000	70,500
Domestic	40,053	51,258	76,736	79,840	72,704
Seed, Feed, Waste	14,300	11,800	12,000	9,600	10,300
Total Usage	169,422	129,895	144,600	128,440	153,504
Ending Stocks	43,000	50,000	75,000	62,000	20,000
Stocks/Use Ratio	25.4 %	38.5 %	51.9 %	48.3 %	13.0 %

Forecasts by STAT Market Research based on data from the USDA and U.S. Department of Commerce

U.S. Black Bean Exports April, 2014

(metric tons)

Crop Year	2011-12	2012-13	2012-13	2013-14	2014
Period	Sep-Aug	Sep-Aug	Sep-Apr	Sep-Apr	Apr
Top Five Buyers					
Mexico	58,588	42,338	30,324	11,707	1,515
Venezuela	0	0	0	2,877	0
Guatemala	2,937	4,662	2,753	2,133	375
Haiti	165	2,913	358	484	0
El Salvador	20	85	43	380	82
Subtotal	61,711	49,998	33,478	17,581	1,971
Percent of Total	94.1%	92.3%	91.8%	91.0%	89.0%
All Buyers					
France	0	0	0	10	0
Germany	9	27	18	19	0
Italy	20	39	39	43	0
Netherlands	14	12	5	9	1
Norway	20	28	28	11	0
Spain	0	0	0	127	78
United Kingdom	363	182	145	257	21
Total W. Europe	426	287	235	475	100
Russia	0	0	0	5	0
Total E. Europe	0	0	0	5	0
Cyprus	218	0	0	0	0
Kuwait	11	0	0	4	0
Qatar	4	0	0	0	0
United Arab Emirates	58	30	7	77	0
Total Middle East	290	30	7	81	0
South Africa	0	0	0	21	0
Total Africa	0	0	0	21	0
China	0	20	20	0	0
Hong Kong	564	312	128	275	18
Japan	231	142	80	145	0
Korea South	117	145	119	108	43
Malaysia	0	0	0	37	0
Philippines	51	84	22	146	0
Singapore	0	18	18	0	0
Total Asia	962	720	386	712	61
Australia	663	407	253	364	62
New Zealand	136	11	0	34	14
Total Pacific	799	418	253	397	76

U.S. Black Bean Exports April, 2014
(metric tons)

Crop Year	2011-12	2012-13	2012-13	2013-14	2014
Period	Sep-Aug	Sep-Aug	Sep-Apr	Sep-Apr	Apr
Brazil	529	0	0	0	0
Chile	0	85	21	0	0
Guyana	7	3	0	0	0
Venezuela	0	0	0	2,877	0
Total S. America	536	88	21	2,877	0
Bahamas	0	7	7	0	0
Belize	83	240	240	0	0
Costa Rica	0	148	128	21	0
Dominican Republic	692	2,139	1,670	13	4
El Salvador	20	85	43	380	82
Guatemala	2,937	4,662	2,753	2,133	375
Haiti	165	2,913	358	484	0
Honduras	2	0	0	0	0
Jamaica	0	1	1	0	0
Leeward Windward Is.	0	0	0	2	0
Mexico	58,588	42,338	30,324	11,707	1,515
Netherlands Antilles	19	42	27	11	4
Panama	34	18	0	0	0
Trinidad	21	3	3	0	0
Turks and Caicos Islands	0	0	0	5	0
Total C. America	62,561	52,596	35,555	14,756	1,979
Total World	65,575	54,140	36,457	19,324	2,216

Source: U.S. Department of Commerce

Red Beans

U.S. Small Red Bean Supply and Demand Estimates

(metric tons, acres)

Year	2010	2011	2012	2013	2014
Acreage	22,900	35,500	40,000	26,000	38,500
Yield (lbs)	2,087	2,076	2,095	2,108	2,129
Production	21,682	33,430	38,011	24,857	37,182
Carryin	7,000	0	2,000	6,000	400
Imports	3,741	4,525	3,822	4,000	5,600
Stocks	32,423	37,955	43,833	34,857	43,182
Disappearance					
Total Exports	4,914	6,786	8,084	10,100	9,100
Domestic	25,610	26,769	27,609	22,257	29,382
Seed, Feed, Waste	1,900	2,400	2,140	2,100	2,300
Total Usage	32,424	35,955	37,833	34,457	40,782
Ending Stocks	0	2,000	6,000	400	2,400
Stocks/Use Ratio	0.0 %	5.6 %	15.9 %	1.2 %	5.9 %

Forecasts by STAT Market Research based on USDA and U.S. Department of Commerce data

Canadian Small Red Bean Exports April, 2014

(metric tons)

Crop Year	2011-12	2012-13	2012-13	2013-14	2014
Period	Aug-Jul	Aug-Jul	Aug-Apr	Aug-Apr	Apr
Top Five Buyers					
Japan	8,644	8,494	6,132	6,228	762
Egypt	0	938	782	4,660	417
Jamaica	372	688	452	940	136
United States	2,508	852	752	567	72
Portugal	0	0	0	408	0
Subtotal	11,524	10,973	8,119	12,803	1,387
Percent of Total	79.7%	75.4%	73.6%	96.3%	95.8%
All Buyers					
United States	2,508	852	752	567	72
Total N. America	2,508	852	752	567	72

Canadian Small Red Bean Exports April, 2014

(metric tons)

Crop Year	2011-12	2012-13	2012-13	2013-14	2014
Period	Aug-Jul	Aug-Jul	Aug-Apr	Aug-Apr	Apr
Austria	4	0	0	3	0
Italy	0	0	0	11	0
Portugal	0	0	0	408	0
Spain	0	114	77	13	0
United Kingdom	170	128	107	60	0
Total W. Europe	174	241	184	495	0
Croatia	0	60	60	0	0
Poland	0	0	0	71	0
Russia	0	0	0	20	0
Total E. Europe	0	60	60	91	0
Egypt	0	938	782	4,660	417
Total Middle East	0	938	782	4,660	417
Algeria	0	120	120	0	0
Equatorial Guinea	0	11	0	0	0
Total Africa	0	131	120	0	0
Japan	8,644	8,494	6,132	6,228	762
Korea South	65	125	102	43	0
Philippines	168	290	185	21	21
Taiwan	1,722	630	630	0	0
Thailand	0	0	0	21	0
Total Asia	10,599	9,539	7,049	6,313	783
Australia	131	242	202	100	40
New Zealand	5	67	53	29	0
U.S. Minor Outlying Islands	499	245	245	0	0
Total Pacific	635	554	500	129	40
Colombia	168	1,377	1,128	100	0
Total S. America	168	1,377	1,128	100	0
Dominica	7	0	0	0	0
Jamaica	372	688	452	940	136
Mexico	0	169	0	0	0
Saint Lucia	3	0	0	0	0
Saint Vincent and the Grenadines	0	0	0	1	0
Total C. America	381	857	452	941	136
Total World	14,465	14,549	11,028	13,296	1,448

Source: Statistics Canada

U.S. Small Red Bean Exports April, 2014

(metric tons)

Crop Year	2011-12	2012-13	2012-13	2013-14	2014
Period	Sep-Aug	Sep-Aug	Sep-Apr	Sep-Apr	Apr
Top Five Buyers					
Jamaica	2,533	3,366	2,254	2,889	515
Japan	2,403	1,870	1,638	1,886	105
Dominican Republic	0	87	1	1,756	651
Portugal	0	0	0	961	0
Canada	2,800	1,406	987	911	221
Subtotal	7,736	6,729	4,880	8,402	1,492
Percent of Total	87.0%	66.8%	76.6%	82.5%	89.8%
All Buyers					
Canada	2,800	1,406	987	911	221
Total N. America	2,800	1,406	987	911	221
France	35	24	24	0	0
Germany	0	41	0	0	0
Italy	113	187	147	40	0
Netherlands	0	0	0	121	0
Norway	49	42	42	41	0
Portugal	0	0	0	961	0
Spain	43	0	0	0	0
Total W. Europe	240	294	213	1,162	0
Japan	2,403	1,870	1,638	1,886	105
Korea South	0	235	194	30	0
Philippines	46	0	0	0	0
Taiwan	20	0	0	61	61
Total Asia	2,469	2,105	1,832	1,977	166
Australia	90	920	374	633	108
French Polynesia	22	60	21	14	0
Total Pacific	112	980	395	647	108
Colombia	0	83	83	0	0
Total S. America	0	83	83	0	0
Bermuda	0	21	21	0	0
Cayman Islands	2	1	1	1	0
Dominican Republic	0	87	1	1,756	651
Guatemala	330	591	260	223	0
Haiti	196	0	0	0	0
Honduras	0	1	1	0	0
Jamaica	2,533	3,366	2,254	2,889	515
Panama	206	1,131	318	621	0
Total C. America	3,267	5,199	2,857	5,490	1,166
Total World	8,888	10,067	6,367	10,187	1,662

Source: U.S. Department of Commerce

Mung Beans

U.S. Mung Bean Exports April, 2014
(metric tons)

Crop Year	2011-12	2012-13	2012-13	2013-14	2014
Period	Sep-Aug	Sep-Aug	Sep-Apr	Sep-Apr	Apr
Top Five Buyers					
Canada	487	284	134	1,616	311
Mexico	8,381	4,435	3,922	958	23
Netherlands	1,458	980	930	932	121
Japan	218	67	67	198	30
China	0	47	0	189	0
Subtotal	10,543	5,813	5,052	3,893	485
Percent of Total	95.6%	90.0%	91.9%	87.0%	91.7%
All Buyers					
Canada	487	284	134	1,616	311
Total N. America	487	284	134	1,616	311
Belgium	72	0	0	18	0
France	0	0	0	61	0
Italy	0	0	0	5	0
Netherlands	1,458	980	930	932	121
Norway	81	0	0	0	0
Spain	0	41	41	0	0
United Kingdom	2	0	0	0	0
Total W. Europe	1,612	1,021	971	1,016	121
Israel	0	32	32	2	0
Jordan	24	0	0	0	0
Qatar	3	0	0	0	0
Saudi Arabia	0	5	0	0	0
Total Middle East	27	37	32	2	0
Algeria	0	54	0	0	0
Angola	1	0	0	0	0
Kenya	0	0	0	18	0
Total Africa	1	54	0	18	0

U.S. Mung Bean Exports April, 2014

(metric tons)

Crop Year	2011-12	2012-13	2012-13	2013-14	2014
Period	Sep-Aug	Sep-Aug	Sep-Apr	Sep-Apr	Apr
China	0	47	0	189	0
Japan	218	67	67	198	30
Philippines	0	8	7	0	0
Sri Lanka	5	20	20	0	0
Taiwan	78	112	112	184	0
Total Asia	301	254	206	571	30
Australia	8	56	0	167	44
New Zealand	1	51	42	19	0
Total Pacific	10	107	42	185	44
Argentina	12	0	0	0	0
Brazil	0	8	8	0	0
Chile	31	44	44	0	0
Peru	0	18	18	0	0
Suriname	86	0	0	0	0
Total S. America	129	70	70	0	0
Barbados	3	0	0	0	0
Costa Rica	1	191	116	88	0
Dominican Republic	0	0	0	19	0
Guatemala	45	0	0	0	0
Jamaica	18	2	2	0	0
Leeward Windward Is.	0	3	3	0	0
Mexico	8,381	4,435	3,922	958	23
Netherlands Antilles	7	0	0	0	0
Panama	4	0	0	0	0
Turks and Caicos Islands	9	0	0	0	0
Total C. America	8,467	4,631	4,043	1,065	23
Total World	11,034	6,458	5,498	4,474	529

Source: U.S. Department of Commerce

Canadian Mung Bean Exports April, 2014
(metric tons)

Crop Year	2011-12	2012-13	2012-13	2013-14	2014
Period	Aug-Jul	Aug-Jul	Aug-Apr	Aug-Apr	Apr
Australia	21	0	0	0	0
Chile	0	43	0	0	0
China	0	0	0	167	0
Hong Kong	0	3	3	0	0
Japan	101	53	0	0	0
Lebanon	5	0	0	0	0
Mexico	56	0	0	0	0
Singapore	0	3	3	0	0
United Kingdom	22	49	0	0	0
United States	2,072	2,455	1,927	1,955	141
Vietnam	0	0	0	31	0
Total World	2,278	2,606	1,933	2,154	141

Source: Statistics Canada

Lima Beans

U.S. Baby Lima Bean Exports April, 2014
(metric tons)

Crop Year	2011-12	2012-13	2012-13	2013-14	2014
Period	Sep-Aug	Sep-Aug	Sep-Apr	Sep-Apr	Apr
Top Five Buyers					
Japan	3,126	4,244	2,619	5,004	850
Italy	86	115	115	347	34
Australia	20	74	74	103	27
United Kingdom	0	96	18	42	0
Argentina	0	0	0	22	0
Subtotal	3,232	4,528	2,826	5,518	910
Percent of Total	88.3%	89.1%	86.1%	99.4%	97.7%
All Buyers					
Belgium	5	0	0	0	0
France	79	0	0	0	0
Germany	2	0	0	0	0
Italy	86	115	115	347	34
Norway	0	3	3	0	0
Portugal	0	14	0	0	0
Spain	0	42	0	0	0
United Kingdom	0	96	18	42	0
Total W. Europe	171	270	136	389	34
Nigeria	4	0	0	0	0
Total Africa	4	0	0	0	0
Hong Kong	28	17	17	0	0
Japan	3,126	4,244	2,619	5,004	850
Malaysia	0	22	22	0	0
Myanmar	0	18	0	0	0
Total Asia	3,154	4,300	2,657	5,004	850
Australia	20	74	74	103	27
New Zealand	44	139	139	0	0
Total Pacific	65	213	213	103	27

U.S. Baby Lima Bean Exports April, 2014

(metric tons)

Crop Year	2011-12	2012-13	2012-13	2013-14	2014
Period	Sep-Aug	Sep-Aug	Sep-Apr	Sep-Apr	Apr
Argentina	0	0	0	22	0
Colombia	23	0	0	1	0
French Guiana	20	0	0	0	0
Peru	0	21	0	0	0
Suriname	29	2	0	4	0
Venezuela	10	0	0	0	0
Total S. America	81	23	0	27	0
Bahamas	6	49	49	0	0
Cayman Islands	0	31	31	4	0
Dominican Republic	2	130	130	0	0
Guatemala	4	23	23	0	0
Jamaica	133	44	44	0	0
Panama	42	0	0	21	21
Trinidad	2	0	0	0	0
Total C. America	188	277	277	26	21
Total World	3,663	5,082	3,283	5,549	932

Source: U.S. Department of Commerce

U.S. Large Lima Bean Exports April, 2014

(metric tons)

Crop Year	2011-12	2012-13	2012-13	2013-14	2014
Period	Sep-Aug	Sep-Aug	Sep-Apr	Sep-Apr	Apr
Top Five Buyers					
Canada	6,447	7,074	4,447	5,968	2,506
United Kingdom	1,940	2,524	2,361	2,132	0
Japan	2,529	3,728	2,365	1,749	199
Bulgaria	0	109	0	656	0
Italy	75	225	130	350	0
Subtotal	10,991	13,660	9,303	10,856	2,705
Percent of Total	89.1%	86.9%	87.9%	94.6%	97.4%
All Buyers					
Canada	6,447	7,074	4,447	5,968	2,506
Total N. America	6,447	7,074	4,447	5,968	2,506

U.S. Large Lima Bean Exports April, 2014

(metric tons)

Crop Year	2011-12	2012-13	2012-13	2013-14	2014
Period	Sep-Aug	Sep-Aug	Sep-Apr	Sep-Apr	Apr
France	21	0	0	21	0
Germany	0	74	0	0	0
Italy	75	225	130	350	0
Netherlands	151	66	52	59	11
Norway	14	16	16	9	0
Portugal	18	6	0	0	0
United Kingdom	1,940	2,524	2,361	2,132	0
Total W. Europe	2,220	2,911	2,558	2,571	11
Bulgaria	0	109	0	656	0
Lithuania	0	67	0	0	0
Russia	62	159	127	0	0
Total E. Europe	62	335	127	656	0
Turkey	0	40	0	0	0
Total Middle East	0	40	0	0	0
French Southern Territories	0	145	0	127	0
Mauritius	450	192	173	18	0
South Africa	0	21	21	0	0
Total Africa	450	357	194	145	0
China	0	53	53	39	0
India	201	417	218	127	36
Japan	2,529	3,728	2,365	1,749	199
Korea South	91	130	127	0	0
Malaysia	0	2	2	2	0
Total Asia	2,820	4,329	2,764	1,917	235
Australia	196	341	207	171	21
New Zealand	4	20	20	2	0
Total Pacific	200	361	227	173	21
Dominican Republic	10	230	224	10	3
Jamaica	85	75	45	41	0
Trinidad	36	0	0	0	0
Total C. America	131	306	269	51	3
Total World	12,329	15,713	10,587	11,481	2,776

Source: U.S. Department of Commerce

Not Elsewhere Specified

Canadian Bean (nes) Exports April, 2014
(metric tons)

Crop Year	2011-12	2012-13	2012-13	2013-14	2014
Period	Aug-Jul	Aug-Jul	Aug-Apr	Aug-Apr	Apr
Top Five Buyers					
United States	58,417	57,881	48,257	42,778	3,873
Angola	7,944	29,172	23,861	16,941	3,706
Italy	2,837	6,553	6,203	10,307	132
Greece	4,824	6,531	5,715	6,123	406
Spain	1,150	1,738	1,502	5,053	247
Subtotal	75,172	101,875	85,539	81,202	8,364
Percent of Total	72.7%	66.1%	65.8%	72.3%	79.2%
All Buyers					
United States	58,417	57,881	48,257	42,778	3,873
Total N. America	58,417	57,881	48,257	42,778	3,873
Austria	23	0	0	15	0
Belgium	211	473	426	2,268	131
France	1,367	493	490	1,670	154
Germany	202	654	610	590	75
Gibraltar	44	0	0	0	0
Greece	4,824	6,531	5,715	6,123	406
Italy	2,837	6,553	6,203	10,307	132
Netherlands	2	947	902	201	80
Portugal	468	5,705	5,580	2,217	25
Spain	1,150	1,738	1,502	5,053	247
Sweden	26	23	23	0	0
Switzerland	43	218	168	271	0
United Kingdom	981	1,122	641	876	65
Total W. Europe	12,178	24,456	22,260	29,592	1,315

Canadian Bean (nes) Exports April, 2014

(metric tons)

Crop Year	2011-12	2012-13	2012-13	2013-14	2014
Period	Aug-Jul	Aug-Jul	Aug-Apr	Aug-Apr	Apr
Albania	0	22	0	25	25
Bosnia and Herzegovina	20	217	217	0	0
Bulgaria	0	342	292	682	133
Croatia	415	1,348	1,248	1,482	20
Czech Republic	25	215	45	264	0
Georgia	0	0	0	75	0
Hungary	0	290	141	245	23
Palestine	20	285	183	211	0
Serbia	40	20	20	0	0
Slovakia	0	50	0	25	0
Slovenia	0	545	501	60	0
Total E. Europe	520	3,334	2,645	3,068	201
Cyprus	0	125	0	44	0
Egypt	0	56	56	0	0
Ethiopia	0	0	0	487	0
Iran	0	3	3	0	0
Israel	213	251	251	600	25
Jordan	28	0	0	0	0
Kuwait	0	3	0	2	0
Lebanon	110	15	0	74	56
Saudi Arabia	0	0	0	82	0
Turkey	630	3,481	3,380	2,662	0
United Arab Emirates	0	27	0	374	299
Yemen	0	0	0	506	0
Total Middle East	982	3,961	3,691	4,831	380
Algeria	374	1,036	1,036	2,793	0
Angola	7,944	29,172	23,861	16,941	3,706
Cape Verde	0	197	73	174	25
Comoros	141	0	0	0	0
Congo	0	50	0	274	0
Congo Democratic Republic (Zaire)	0	249	249	0	0
Liberia	0	0	0	25	0
South Africa	0	314	308	167	0
Total Africa	8,459	31,019	25,527	20,374	3,731

Canadian Bean (nes) Exports April, 2014

(metric tons)

Crop Year	2011-12	2012-13	2012-13	2013-14	2014
Period	Aug-Jul	Aug-Jul	Aug-Apr	Aug-Apr	Apr
China	0	338	184	0	0
Hong Kong	0	1	1	0	0
India	0	550	550	444	0
Japan	4,500	6,788	5,214	3,972	252
Korea South	0	419	359	22	0
Malaysia	68	0	0	23	0
Pakistan	0	276	276	38	0
Philippines	3	0	0	0	0
Singapore	0	3	3	0	0
Total Asia	4,571	8,375	6,586	4,498	252
Australia	919	924	677	649	98
New Zealand	422	537	460	221	8
U.S. Minor Outlying Islands	467	299	299	25	0
Total Pacific	1,808	1,760	1,436	895	106
Brazil	150	0	0	0	0
Chile	472	3,393	2,454	848	199
Colombia	0	191	191	25	25
Peru	344	285	185	50	0
Uruguay	0	22	0	0	0
Venezuela	149	206	206	1,994	0
Total S. America	1,114	4,097	3,036	2,917	224
Antigua and Barbuda	0	5	4	3	0
Aruba	1	1	1	2	0
Bermuda	1	0	0	0	0
Cuba	0	4,249	4,247	0	0
Dominica	41	57	39	71	6
Dominican Republic	1,584	3,213	2,841	1,042	0
El Salvador	0	80	80	0	0
Grenada	0	2	2	0	0
Guatemala	184	0	0	220	220
Haiti	205	435	124	0	0
Jamaica	2	24	24	0	0
Mexico	13,254	11,138	9,077	1,951	230
Panama	19	22	22	16	0
Saint Lucia	0	0	0	4	4
Trinidad	104	105	91	55	25
Total C. America	15,395	19,332	16,553	3,364	485
Total World	103,445	154,215	129,992	112,316	10,566

Source: Statistics Canada

U.S. Bean (nes) Exports April, 2014

(metric tons)

Crop Year	2011-12	2012-13	2012-13	2013-14	2014
Period	Sep-Aug	Sep-Aug	Sep-Apr	Sep-Apr	Apr
Top Five Buyers					
Canada	8,831	15,513	12,549	9,286	1,469
Australia	2,241	961	632	786	103
Turkey	0	0	0	709	60
Mexico	2,257	1,481	1,163	614	246
New Zealand	368	689	263	456	0
Subtotal	13,697	18,643	14,606	11,850	1,878
Percent of Total	67.8%	80.9%	83.3%	73.3%	85.7%
All Buyers					
Canada	8,831	15,513	12,549	9,286	1,469
Total N. America	8,831	15,513	12,549	9,286	1,469
Denmark	18	72	54	36	0
France	79	336	335	288	20
Germany	457	49	0	0	0
Greece	18	12	12	0	0
Italy	150	156	20	362	0
Netherlands	58	108	59	212	24
Spain	50	0	0	200	0
Sweden	0	24	24	0	0
United Kingdom	434	165	85	57	0
Total W. Europe	1,264	922	588	1,156	43
Albania	0	0	0	82	0
Bulgaria	0	0	0	53	53
Total E. Europe	0	0	0	134	53
Bahrain	30	70	49	43	0
Cyprus	116	0	0	40	0
Israel	99	79	79	64	0
Jordan	92	73	73	75	0
Turkey	0	0	0	709	60
United Arab Emirates	33	3	0	0	0
Total Middle East	370	225	201	931	60
Algeria	65	0	0	0	0
Angola	0	21	21	0	0
Kenya	3	0	0	0	0
Malawi	668	0	0	0	0
Mauritius	70	182	91	0	0
Morocco	1	0	0	0	0
South Africa	237	31	11	75	0
Total Africa	1,043	233	122	75	0

U.S. Bean (nes) Exports April, 2014
(metric tons)

Crop Year Period	2011-12 Sep-Aug	2012-13 Sep-Aug	2012-13 Sep-Apr	2013-14 Sep-Apr	2014 Apr
Cambodia	111	0	0	0	0
Hong Kong	197	171	130	69	11
India	440	454	181	0	0
Japan	545	228	224	442	21
Macau	2	0	0	0	0
Malaysia	173	149	113	73	0
Myanmar	0	36	0	0	0
Pakistan	154	0	0	0	0
Singapore	0	36	36	18	0
Sri Lanka	38	0	0	0	0
Taiwan	7	0	0	0	0
Thailand	63	54	54	80	0
Total Asia	1,730	1,128	739	682	33
Australia	2,241	961	632	786	103
French Polynesia	106	92	54	59	0
New Zealand	368	689	263	456	0
South Georgia and the South Sandwich Islands	0	0	0	14	0
Total Pacific	2,715	1,742	949	1,315	103
Argentina	94	23	23	88	36
Bolivia	1	0	0	0	0
Chile	18	4	4	429	72
Colombia	2	14	6	8	0
French Guiana	308	359	297	247	0
Peru	1	0	0	51	0
Suriname	0	1	1	0	0
Venezuela	121	48	0	0	0
Total S. America	545	448	331	823	108

U.S. Bean (nes) Exports April, 2014
(metric tons)

Crop Year	2011-12	2012-13	2012-13	2013-14	2014
Period	Sep-Aug	Sep-Aug	Sep-Apr	Sep-Apr	Apr
Bahamas	221	294	183	164	48
Belize	193	103	103	107	0
Bermuda	1	0	0	0	0
Cayman Islands	4	0	0	0	0
Costa Rica	31	57	15	11	9
Dominican Republic	90	166	144	0	0
Guatemala	59	0	0	0	0
Haiti	17	91	45	136	0
Honduras	25	0	0	0	0
Jamaica	431	184	116	2	0
Leeward Windward Is.	263	324	167	232	20
Mexico	2,257	1,481	1,163	614	246
Netherlands Antilles	103	74	74	0	0
Nicaragua	0	0	0	230	0
Panama	9	48	48	52	0
Trinidad	8	11	0	212	0
Turks and Caicos Islands	1	5	5	0	0
Total C. America	3,711	2,837	2,063	1,760	322
Total World	20,209	23,047	17,542	16,161	2,191

Source: U.S. Department of Commerce

Australian Beans (nes) Exports April, 2014
(metric tons)

Crop Year	2011-12	2012-13	2012-13	2013-14	2014
Period	Nov-Oct	Nov-Oct	Nov-Apr	Nov-Apr	Apr
Top Five Buyers					
Singapore	183	148	64	80	0
Taiwan	0	0	0	63	0
Subtotal	183	148	64	143	0
Percent of Total	48.2%	25.9%	13.3%	95.4%	0.0%
All Buyers					
Canada	6	0	0	0	0
Total N. America	6	0	0	0	0
Egypt	0	372	372	0	0
Yemen	23	0	0	0	0
Total Middle East	23	372	372	0	0
South Africa	44	0	0	0	0
Total Africa	44	0	0	0	0
India	25	43	43	5	0
Malaysia	0	4	1	0	0
Philippines	88	0	0	0	0
Singapore	183	148	64	80	0
Taiwan	0	0	0	63	0
Thailand	7	5	3	2	1
Total Asia	303	199	111	150	1
Papua New Guinea	4	0	0	0	0
Total Pacific	4	0	0	0	0
Total World	379	571	483	150	1

Source: Australia Bureau of Statistics

Other Beans

U.S. Great Northern Bean Supply and Demand Estimates
(metric tons, acres)

Year	2010	2011	2012	2013	2014
Acreage	78,500	61,800	55,900	75,500	105,500
Yield (lbs)	1,787	1,935	2,186	2,007	1,948
Production	63,640	54,250	55,430	68,720	93,236
Carryin	21,000	29,000	19,000	2,500	1,300
Stocks	84,640	83,251	74,429	71,220	94,536
Disappearance					
Europe	7,520	11,191	21,302	26,000	27,400
Americas	721	588	2,643	1,200	2,400
Other	4,817	8,707	11,475	10,300	13,900
Total Exports	13,058	20,486	35,420	37,500	43,700
Domestic	39,778	41,230	33,451	27,635	40,293
Seed, Feed, Waste	2,803	2,536	3,058	4,785	3,543
Total Usage	55,640	64,251	71,929	69,920	87,536
Ending Stocks	29,000	19,000	2,500	1,300	7,000
Stocks/Use Ratio	52.1 %	29.6 %	3.5 %	1.9 %	8.0 %

Forecasts by STAT Market Research based on USDA and U.S. Department of Commerce data

U.S. Great Northern Bean Exports April, 2014

(metric tons)

Crop Year	2011-12	2012-13	2012-13	2013-14	2014
Period	Sep-Aug	Sep-Aug	Sep-Apr	Sep-Apr	Apr
Top Five Buyers					
Spain	48	1,316	385	7,731	821
France	6,524	5,058	4,338	5,571	838
Algeria	0	5,818	3,479	4,780	0
Portugal	0	3,620	1,829	3,978	769
Turkey	1,821	8,598	7,730	2,964	407
Subtotal	8,393	24,409	17,761	25,024	2,835
Percent of Total	41.0%	68.9%	68.1%	80.9%	86.1%
All Buyers					
Austria	0	61	40	0	0
Belgium	1,224	988	948	947	0
Denmark	3	3	1	0	0
France	6,524	5,058	4,338	5,571	838
Germany	404	638	615	23	0
Greece	187	502	422	43	0
Italy	0	20	0	206	0
Netherlands	155	136	136	120	0
Portugal	0	3,620	1,829	3,978	769
Spain	48	1,316	385	7,731	821
Sweden	0	23	23	39	0
United Kingdom	0	0	0	20	0
Total W. Europe	8,546	12,365	8,737	18,676	2,428
Russia	825	340	272	968	0
Total E. Europe	825	340	272	968	0
Israel	0	43	23	244	0
Turkey	1,821	8,598	7,730	2,964	407
United Arab Emirates	46	45	45	0	0
Yemen	3,695	211	0	0	0
Total Middle East	5,562	8,896	7,798	3,208	407
Algeria	0	5,818	3,479	4,780	0
Benin	0	1,000	1,000	0	0
Total Africa	0	6,817	4,479	4,780	0
Hong Kong	0	49	49	0	0
Japan	1,036	1,091	642	471	61
Korea South	0	0	0	21	0
Malaysia	2,866	1,709	1,162	1,041	210
Philippines	406	660	265	612	125
Singapore	0	120	0	0	0
Total Asia	4,309	3,628	2,118	2,146	396

U.S. Great Northern Bean Exports April, 2014

(metric tons)

Crop Year	2011-12	2012-13	2012-13	2013-14	2014
Period	Sep-Aug	Sep-Aug	Sep-Apr	Sep-Apr	Apr
Australia	533	681	449	290	59
New Zealand	124	51	43	16	0
Total Pacific	657	732	491	306	59
Argentina	2	0	0	0	0
Total S. America	2	0	0	0	0
Dominican Republic	3	410	409	2	1
Haiti	0	23	23	0	0
Mexico	583	2,210	1,748	840	0
Panama	0	0	0	3	0
Total C. America	586	2,643	2,179	845	1
Total World	20,486	35,420	26,074	30,930	3,291

Source: U.S. Department of Commerce

U.S. Pink Bean Supply and Demand Estimates

(metric tons, acres)

Year	2010	2011	2012	2013	2014
Acreage	33,000	21,100	29,400	23,500	31,200
Yield (lbs)	1,776	1,934	2,082	2,026	1,994
Production	26,581	18,507	27,760	21,591	28,213
Carryin	1,000	3,000	1,000	2,200	1,000
Stocks	27,580	21,506	28,760	23,791	29,213
Disappearance					
Total Exports	540	1,569	1,314	940	1,500
Domestic	22,641	17,537	23,747	20,305	22,300
Seed, Feed, Waste	1,400	1,400	1,500	1,546	1,613
Total Usage	24,581	20,506	26,561	22,791	25,413
Ending Stocks	3,000	1,000	2,200	1,000	3,800
Stocks/Use Ratio	12.2 %	4.9 %	8.3 %	4.4 %	15.0 %

Forecasts by STAT Market Research based on USDA and U.S. Department of Commerce data

U.S. Pink Bean Exports April, 2014
(metric tons)

Crop Year Period	2011-12 Sep-Aug	2012-13 Sep-Aug	2012-13 Sep-Apr	2013-14 Sep-Apr	2014 Apr
Dominican Republic	476	579	511	16	0
France	1	35	30	87	25
Honduras	2	1	1	0	0
India	0	141	141	0	0
Jamaica	0	0	0	2	0
Japan	21	0	0	0	0
Leeward Windward Is.	13	47	14	44	0
Mexico	875	190	150	0	0
Netherlands	6	0	0	0	0
Netherlands Antilles	17	35	19	2	0
Norway	15	8	8	0	0
Panama	0	42	0	40	0
Saudi Arabia	5	0	0	0	0
Suriname	25	0	0	0	0
Trinidad	113	180	94	387	23
Total World	1,569	1,257	968	578	48

Source: U.S. Department of Commerce

U.S. Cranberry Bean Exports April, 2014
(metric tons)

Crop Year Period	2011-12 Sep-Aug	2012-13 Sep-Aug	2012-13 Sep-Apr	2013-14 Sep-Apr	2014 Apr
Top Five Buyers					
Spain	0	233	78	2,081	200
Dominican Republic	5	9	9	1,252	0
Italy	1,403	456	456	1,188	433
Taiwan	131	758	640	580	154
Australia	495	71	71	107	0
Subtotal	2,034	1,527	1,253	5,208	787
Percent of Total	57.8%	75.0%	73.4%	97.2%	97.7%
All Buyers					
Austria	0	52	52	0	0
Italy	1,403	456	456	1,188	433
Spain	0	233	78	2,081	200
Total W. Europe	1,403	741	586	3,270	633

U.S. Cranberry Bean Exports April, 2014

(metric tons)

Crop Year	2011-12	2012-13	2012-13	2013-14	2014
Period	Sep-Aug	Sep-Aug	Sep-Apr	Sep-Apr	Apr
Slovenia	0	21	21	0	0
Yugoslavia	0	60	60	0	0
Total E. Europe	0	81	81	0	0
Israel	74	0	0	0	0
Jordan	0	0	0	24	0
Total Middle East	74	0	0	24	0
Nigeria	5	0	0	0	0
South Africa	14	64	44	0	0
Total Africa	19	64	44	0	0
China	267	43	22	0	0
Hong Kong	152	5	5	0	0
Japan	431	8	8	17	0
Korea South	194	84	84	32	0
Philippines	22	0	0	0	0
Taiwan	131	758	640	580	154
Thailand	235	139	139	0	0
Total Asia	1,431	1,038	898	629	154
Australia	495	71	71	107	0
New Zealand	0	0	0	23	19
Total Pacific	495	71	71	130	19
Chile	0	0	0	2	0
Total S. America	0	0	0	2	0
Costa Rica	8	0	0	0	0
Dominican Republic	5	9	9	1,252	0
Leeward Windward Is.	0	0	0	50	0
Netherlands Antilles	0	11	0	0	0
Panama	4	18	18	0	0
Trinidad	78	2	2	0	0
Total C. America	96	41	29	1,301	0
Total World	3,518	2,036	1,708	5,356	805

Source: U.S. Department of Commerce

U.S. Bambara Bean Exports April, 2014

(metric tons)

Crop Year	2011-12	2012-13	2012-13	2013-14	2014
Period	Sep-Aug	Sep-Aug	Sep-Apr	Sep-Apr	Apr
Argentina	0	0	0	8	0
Bolivia	0	5	0	0	0
Canada	5	40	24	35	12
Mexico	0	8	0	0	0
Netherlands Antilles	7	25	25	0	0
Norway	4	0	0	0	0
Total World	16	78	49	44	12

Source: U.S. Department of Commerce

Australian Adzuki Bean Exports April, 2014

(metric tons)

Crop Year	2011-12	2012-13	2012-13	2013-14	2014
Period	Nov-Oct	Nov-Oct	Nov-Apr	Nov-Apr	Apr
Japan	62	122	42	124	0
Malaysia	0	40	40	162	72
New Zealand	42	0	0	25	20
Taiwan	917	1,365	1,097	337	0
Total World	1,021	1,527	1,179	648	92

Source: Australia Bureau of Statistics

U.S. Blackeye Cowpea Supply and Demand Estimates

(metric tons, acres)

Year	2010	2011	2012	2013	2014
Acreage	34,800	24,600	37,400	42,100	33,100
Yield (lbs)	1,681	1,370	1,460	1,520	1,448
Production	26,535	15,286	24,766	29,030	21,745
Carryin	500	500	3,000	6,000	3,000
Imports	2,229	19,530	11,325	2,400	6,100
Stocks	29,264	35,316	39,091	37,430	30,846
Disappearance					
Total Exports	1,720	419	836	980	1,070
Domestic	25,645	30,597	30,548	31,750	26,576
Seed, Feed, Waste	1,400	1,300	1,706	1,700	1,700
Total Usage	28,765	32,316	33,090	34,430	29,346
Ending Stocks	500	3,000	6,000	3,000	1,500
Stocks/Use Ratio	1.7 %	9.3 %	18.1 %	8.7 %	5.1 %

Forecasts by STAT Market Research based on USDA and U.S. Department of Commerce data

U.S. Blackeye Cowpea Exports April, 2014

(metric tons)

Crop Year	2011-12	2012-13	2012-13	2013-14	2014
Period	Sep-Aug	Sep-Aug	Sep-Apr	Sep-Apr	Apr
Top Five Buyers					
Mexico	22,175	8,253	5,950	1,661	0
Netherlands	259	362	305	151	31
Malaysia	0	142	108	112	0
Australia	0	0	0	98	42
Korea South	0	54	54	91	0
Subtotal	22,434	8,811	6,417	2,112	73
Percent of Total	99.3%	96.9%	97.3%	87.8%	61.0%
All Buyers					
Canada	0	61	56	48	0
Total N. America	0	61	56	48	0
Netherlands	259	362	305	151	31
Total W. Europe	259	362	305	151	31
United Arab Emirates	0	0	0	76	0
Total Middle East	0	0	0	76	0
Hong Kong	0	38	0	81	45
India	0	41	0	0	0
Japan	17	0	0	0	0
Korea South	0	54	54	91	0
Malaysia	0	142	108	112	0
Singapore	0	39	39	0	0
Total Asia	17	315	201	283	45
Australia	0	0	0	98	42
New Zealand	38	0	0	0	0
South Georgia and the South Sandwich Islands	0	22	22	0	0
Total Pacific	38	22	22	98	42
Barbados	87	70	58	42	0
Jamaica	0	5	2	43	0
Mexico	22,175	8,253	5,950	1,661	0
Netherlands Antilles	4	3	2	4	1
Trinidad	15	0	0	0	0
Total C. America	22,280	8,331	6,012	1,750	1
Total World	22,594	9,090	6,596	2,405	120

Source: U.S. Department of Commerce

Estimates

U.S. Per Capita Bean Consumption Forecast
(pounds per person per year)

	2010	2011	2012	2013	2014
Pinto	3.48	1.73	2.71	2.64	2.62
Navy	0.84	0.38	0.86	0.73	0.68
Great Northern	0.21	0.36	0.17	0.23	0.23
All Kidney	0.49	0.45	0.41	0.49	0.46
Dark Red	0.23	0.23	0.17	0.22	0.21
Light Red	0.26	0.22	0.24	0.27	0.26
Black	0.37	0.89	0.73	0.61	0.62
Lima	0.11	0.14	0.07	0.11	0.11
Baby Lima	0.06	0.08	0.04	0.05	0.05
Large Lima	0.05	0.06	0.03	0.06	0.06
Small Red	0.20	0.24	0.19	0.23	0.22
Chickpea	0.44	0.42	0.63	0.44	0.46
Blackeye	0.17	0.18	0.14	0.18	0.18
Pink	0.16	0.17	0.14	0.16	0.16
Cranberry		0.01	0.01	0.01	0.01
Other	0.54	0.54	0.43	0.40	0.43
Total	7.01	5.51	6.49	6.23	6.19
Usage Conversions (metric tons)					
Inferred Use	986,086	782,323	931,587	902,204	905,516
5-year Av	857,450	892,152	873,040	885,162	888,621

BASED on USDA ERS data

USDA NASS Bean Production Estimates By State

(metric tons)

Production	2010	2011	2012	2013	2014
Arizona	11,001	7,031	12,565	7,620	13,904
California	66,298	49,125	59,149	52,164	44,709
Colorado	56,881	26,535	37,558	24,494	32,196
Idaho	115,486	85,276	137,168	106,867	120,866
Kansas	10,614	4,627	7,167	3,901	5,614
Michigan	191,872	152,409	159,938	148,326	154,717
Minnesota	138,914	103,465	140,751	106,142	136,111
Montana	16,298	12,247	21,138	20,548	31,467
N. Dakota	520,412	224,077	528,894	321,827	413,557
Nebraska	144,834	95,255	144,834	124,739	163,857
New Mexico	14,585	12,565	9,798	8,800	9,768
New York	12,774	7,484	8,255	7,258	5,873
Oregon	6,760	6,985	11,703	8,392	8,349
South Dakota	10,456	7,212	12,066	10,433	7,904
Texas	10,428	3,629	6,169	16,602	10,129
Utah	N/A	N/A	N/A	N/A	N/A
Washington	62,415	66,361	100,699	94,121	108,250
Wisconsin	6,046	4,990	4,581	4,445	5,625
Wyoming	46,476	32,931	45,677	43,999	50,690
Total	1,442,549	902,204	1,448,109	1,110,678	1,323,585

USDA NASS Bean Production Estimates By State
(acres)

Seeded Area	2010	2011	2012	2013	2014
Arizona	13,000	8,500	13,500	10,000	16,000
California	63,500	57,500	58,500	50,000	45,000
Colorado	70,000	38,000	50,000	39,000	45,000
Idaho	135,000	95,000	145,000	125,000	135,000
Kansas	9,500	6,500	8,000	5,000	6,000
Michigan	236,000	170,000	200,000	175,000	185,000
Minnesota	185,000	140,000	160,000	125,000	170,000
Montana	18,800	15,000	32,000	24,000	38,000
N. Dakota	800,000	410,000	700,000	440,000	620,000
Nebraska	170,000	110,000	145,000	130,000	180,000
New Mexico	13,800	12,500	9,800	10,000	9,800
New York	15,000	12,000	10,000	9,000	8,000
Oregon	7,100	6,400	10,500	8,300	8,000
South Dakota	12,500	10,200	13,000	12,000	9,000
Texas	21,000	9,000	22,000	33,000	23,000
Utah	N/A	N/A	N/A	N/A	N/A
Washington	86,000	77,000	115,000	115,000	130,000
Wisconsin	6,200	5,300	5,200	5,400	6,200
Wyoming	49,000	35,000	45,000	39,000	52,000
Total	1,911,400	1,217,900	1,742,500	1,354,700	1,686,000

USDA NASS Bean Production Estimates By State

(acres)

Harvested Area	2010	2011	2012	2013	2014
Arizona	12,900	8,200	13,400	10,000	15,800
California	63,000	57,000	57,500	49,500	44,200
Colorado	66,000	37,000	45,000	36,000	42,000
Idaho	134,000	94,000	144,000	124,000	133,900
Kansas	9,000	6,000	7,500	4,800	5,600
Michigan	235,000	168,000	197,000	172,000	182,400
Minnesota	175,000	135,000	155,000	120,000	162,200
Montana	17,700	14,800	31,100	23,600	36,900
N. Dakota	770,000	380,000	685,000	430,000	595,900
Nebraska	155,000	105,000	133,000	117,000	164,200
New Mexico	13,800	12,400	9,800	9,500	9,700
New York	14,900	11,800	9,500	8,800	7,800
Oregon	6,900	6,400	10,500	8,200	7,900
South Dakota	11,300	9,000	12,900	11,500	8,500
Texas	19,000	8,000	17,000	30,000	20,300
Utah	N/A	N/A	N/A	N/A	N/A
Washington	86,000	77,000	115,000	114,000	129,700
Wisconsin	6,200	5,300	5,200	5,400	6,200
Wyoming	47,000	33,000	42,000	37,000	48,800
Total	1,842,700	1,167,900	1,690,400	1,311,300	1,622,000

USDA NASS Bean Production Estimates By State

(pounds per acre)

Yield	2010	2011	2012	2013	2014
Arizona	1,880	1,890	2,067	1,680	1,940
California	2,320	1,900	2,268	2,323	2,230
Colorado	1,900	1,581	1,840	1,500	1,690
Idaho	1,900	2,000	2,100	1,900	1,990
Kansas	2,600	1,700	2,107	1,792	2,210
Michigan	1,800	2,000	1,790	1,901	1,870
Minnesota	1,750	1,690	2,002	1,950	1,850
Montana	2,030	1,824	1,498	1,919	1,880
N. Dakota	1,490	1,300	1,702	1,650	1,530
Nebraska	2,060	2,000	2,401	2,350	2,200
New Mexico	2,330	2,234	2,204	2,042	2,220
New York	1,890	1,398	1,916	1,818	1,660
Oregon	2,160	2,406	2,457	2,256	2,330
South Dakota	2,040	1,767	2,062	2,000	2,050
Texas	1,210	1,000	800	1,220	1,100
Utah	N/A	N/A	N/A	N/A	N/A
Washington	1,600	1,900	1,930	1,820	1,840
Wisconsin	2,150	2,075	1,942	1,815	2,000
Wyoming	2,180	2,200	2,398	2,622	2,290
Total	1,726	1,703	1,889	1,867	1,790

Based on USDA data.

USDA NASS Dry Edible Bean Estimates by Variety

(metric tons)

Production	2010	2011	2012	2013	2014
Large Lima	18,099	10,523	10,297	7,439	7,531
Baby Lima	13,789	10,705	13,699	9,117	8,332
Navy	216,184	147,328	222,535	154,314	210,704
Great Northern	63,640	54,250	55,430	68,720	93,236
Small White	3,221	1,315	1,497	N/A	1,229
Pinto	626,599	266,443	613,898	384,922	506,187
L. Red Kidney	43,817	29,121	36,378	38,329	39,596
D. Red Kidney	37,785	35,834	41,051	37,875	45,298
Pink	26,581	18,507	27,760	21,591	28,213
Small Red	21,682	33,430	38,011	24,857	37,182
Cranberry	2,994	3,084	3,130	2,404	2,871
Black	211,422	136,896	169,600	115,440	111,504
Blackeye	26,535	15,286	24,766	29,030	21,745
Garbanzo	87,952	99,882	151,139	157,353	153,905
Other	42,250	39,599	38,919	59,285	157,069
Total	1,442,549	902,204	1,448,109	1,110,678	1,424,602

USDA NASS Dry Edible Bean Estimates by Variety

(acres)

Seeded Area	2010	2011	2012	2013	2014
Large Lima	17,500	9,600	9,700	6,700	7,000
Baby Lima	12,200	12,600	12,900	6,800	7,600
Navy	279,500	204,400	262,800	174,200	262,700
Great Northern	78,500	61,800	55,900	75,500	105,500
Small White	2,700	1,100	1,200	N/A	1,000
Pinto	842,700	386,700	729,700	485,100	668,400
Light Red Kidney	53,100	37,200	40,200	43,200	46,400
Dark Red Kidney	48,500	48,800	46,200	46,700	55,700
Pink	33,000	21,100	29,400	23,500	31,200
Small Red	22,900	35,500	40,000	26,000	38,500
Cranberry	4,400	4,300	4,700	4,100	4,400
Black	284,000	183,900	216,800	143,100	141,700
Blackeye	34,800	24,600	37,400	42,100	33,100
Garbanzo	146,000	135,800	207,900	215,700	217,800
Other	51,700	50,500	48,000	62,000	65,000
Total	1,911,500	1,217,900	1,742,800	1,354,700	1,686,000

USDA NASS Dry Edible Bean Estimates by Variety

(pounds per acre)

Yield	2010	2011	2012	2013	2014
Large Lima	2,280	2,417	2,340	2,448	2,372
Baby Lima	2,492	1,873	2,341	2,956	2,417
Navy	1,705	1,589	1,867	1,953	1,768
Great Northern	1,787	1,935	2,186	2,007	1,948
Small White	2,630	2,636	2,750	N/A	2,709
Pinto	1,639	1,519	1,855	1,749	1,670
Light Red Kidney	1,819	1,726	1,995	1,956	1,881
Dark Red Kidney	1,718	1,619	1,959	1,788	1,793
Pink	1,776	1,934	2,082	2,026	1,994
Small Red	2,087	2,076	2,095	2,108	2,129
Cranberry	1,500	1,581	1,468	1,293	1,438
Black	1,641	1,641	1,725	1,778	1,735
Blackeye	1,681	1,370	1,460	1,520	1,448
Garbanzo	1,328	1,622	1,603	1,608	1,558
Other	1,802	1,729	1,788	2,108	5,327

Based on USDA data.

NAFTA Region Bean Situation and Outlook

(acres, metric tons)

Area (acres)	2010	2011	2012	2013	2014
Canada	331,100	197,881	300,000	245,000	282,000
United States	1,765,400	1,082,100	1,534,600	1,131,700	1,318,700
Mexico	3,749,000	2,278,000	3,852,000	4,230,000	3,714,000
Total	5,845,500	3,557,981	5,686,600	5,606,700	5,314,700
Production (MT)					
Canada					
- Colored	151,300	116,300	158,700	140,700	146,000
- White	102,300	46,100	115,600	65,400	84,000
Cdn Total	253,600	162,400	274,300	206,100	230,000
United States					
- Pinto	626,599	266,443	613,898	386,601	448,840
- Black	211,422	136,896	169,600	113,853	96,283
- Navy	216,184	147,328	222,535	153,134	189,529
- Great Northern	63,640	54,250	55,430	68,448	78,440
- Other	237,155	197,083	235,538	217,964	461,908
U.S. Total	1,355,000	802,000	1,297,000	940,000	1,275,000
Mexico	963,000	626,000	1,063,000	1,135,000	1,069,000
Total Production	2,571,600	1,590,400	2,634,300	2,051,880	2,574,000
Opening Stocks	359,000	472,000	96,000	349,000	321,000
Total Supply	2,930,600	2,062,400	2,730,300	2,400,880	2,895,000
Exports	349,000	327,000	388,000	351,000	334,000
Domestic	2,109,600	1,639,400	1,993,300	1,728,880	2,260,000
Average Domestic	2,273,000	2,192,000	2,040,000	1,957,000	1,884,000

BASED on data from USDA, Statistics Canada and STAT Publishing. Excludes chickpeas.

Lentils

World Lentil Supply and Demand Situation
(hectares, metric tons, kilograms)

	2010	2011	2012	2013	2014
Area (hectares)	4,309,000	4,302,000	4,367,000	3,814,000	3,777,000
Yield (kg/ha)	1,157	1,023	1,010	999	1,093
Production	4,985,000	4,401,000	4,409,000	3,811,000	4,128,000
Carry-in	97,000	1,015,000	1,009,000	371,000	267,000
Supply	5,082,000	5,416,000	5,418,000	4,182,000	4,395,000
Trade	1,994,000	1,805,000	2,309,000	2,276,000	2,137,000
Inferred Use	4,067,000	4,407,000	5,047,000	3,915,000	4,128,000
Ending Stock	1,015,000	1,009,000	371,000	267,000	267,000
Stock-Use Ratio	25.0%	22.9%	7.4%	6.8%	6.5%
Per Capita Use (kg)	0.594	0.636	0.721	0.553	0.583

Estimates by STAT Publishing based data from the FAO, USDA, Statistics Canada, ABARES, and other entities.

Canadian Lentil Supply and Demand Estimates
(metric tons, acres)

Year	2010	2011	2012	2013	2014
Area (acres)	3,445,000	2,557,800	2,515,000	2,393,000	2,860,000
Yield (lbs)	1,283	1,356	1,348	1,732	1,421
Production	2,004,800	1,573,500	1,537,900	1,880,500	1,844,000
Carry In	40,000	830,000	860,000	307,000	182,000
Imports	27,755	12,076	20,512	7,000	15,000
Stocks	2,072,555	2,415,576	2,418,413	2,194,500	2,041,000
Disappearance					
Aug-Apr Exports	896,658	872,896	1,130,795	1,217,590	N/A
Percent of Forecast	81.1 %	76.0 %	69.0 %	75.9 %	N/A
Europe	47,587	45,937	46,774	59,700	48,700
Mediterranean	301,470	281,193	256,195	350,300	309,300
South America	161,025	180,886	178,692	173,000	185,600
N/C America	52,375	77,331	62,965	69,000	66,900
Pacific Rim	287,623	309,740	811,367	637,400	689,400
Arab/Africa	255,841	252,918	283,053	315,500	309,100
Total Export	1,105,920	1,148,004	1,639,046	1,604,900	1,609,000
Seed	87,200	87,900	80,800	94,600	101,700
Other Domestic	49,435	319,671	391,566	313,000	167,300
Total Usage	1,242,555	1,555,576	2,111,413	2,012,500	1,878,000
Ending Stock	830,000	860,000	307,000	182,000	163,000
Stock/Use	66.8 %	55.3 %	14.5 %	9.0 %	8.7 %

Forecasts by STAT Market Research based on data from Statistics Canada.

World Lentil Production Summary

(hectares, metric tons, kilograms)

Area (hectares)	2010	2011	2012	2013	2014
Australia	166,000	173,000	164,000	168,000	160,000
Canada	1,394,000	1,035,000	1,018,000	968,000	1,157,000
United States	112,000	171,000	272,000	177,000	192,000
Turkey	234,000	315,000	237,000	249,000	300,000
Syria	131,000	140,000	145,000	65,000	35,000
Morocco	41,000	58,000	49,000	46,000	47,000
India	1,479,000	1,597,000	1,600,000	1,330,000	1,064,000
Bangladesh	77,000	83,000	85,000	78,000	79,000
Pakistan	24,000	26,000	27,000	28,000	24,000
Other	651,000	704,000	770,000	705,000	719,000
Total	4,309,000	4,302,000	4,367,000	3,814,000	3,777,000
Production (MT)	2010	2011	2012	2013	2014
Australia	306,000	307,000	274,000	253,000	264,000
Canada	2,005,000	1,574,000	1,538,000	1,881,000	1,844,000
United States	393,000	215,000	240,000	228,000	185,000
Turkey	447,000	405,000	438,000	300,000	463,000
Syria	77,000	112,000	115,000	15,000	11,000
Morocco	28,000	45,000	22,000	32,000	31,000
India	1,032,000	944,000	950,000	400,000	586,000
Bangladesh	71,000	80,000	85,000	74,000	75,000
Pakistan	11,000	13,000	15,000	10,000	11,000
Other	615,000	706,000	732,000	618,000	658,000
Total	4,985,000	4,401,000	4,409,000	3,811,000	4,128,000
Yields (kg per hectare)	2010	2011	2012	2013	2014
Australia	1,843	1,775	1,671	1,506	1,650
Canada	1,438	1,521	1,511	1,943	1,594
United States	3,509	1,257	882	1,288	964
Turkey	1,910	1,286	1,848	1,205	1,543
Syria	588	800	793	231	314
Morocco	683	776	449	696	660
India	698	591	594	301	551
Bangladesh	922	964	1,000	949	949
Pakistan	458	500	556	357	458
Other	945	1,003	951	877	915
World Yield	1,157	1,023	1,010	999	1,093

Projections by STAT Market Research based on data from Statistics Canada, ABARE, USDA, FAO

U.S. Lentil Supply and Demand Estimates

(metric tons, acres)

Year	2010	2011	2012	2013	2014
Acreage	658,000	428,000	463,000	362,000	320,000
Yield (lbs)	1,316	1,106	1,145	1,386	1,277
Production	392,679	214,642	240,497	227,660	185,400
Other	12,817	8,366	9,012	8,692	7,635
Carry In	5,000	86,000	69,000	21,000	48,000
Stocks	410,495	309,008	318,510	257,352	241,035
Disappearance					
Sep-Apr Exports	178,431	121,671	175,958	105,732	N/A
Percent of Forecast	83.4 %	70.9 %	75.9 %	70.5 %	N/A
Europe	21,824	23,982	9,468	4,000	10,000
Mediterranean	35,376	32,060	40,983	40,000	28,000
Americas	55,245	28,818	33,299	28,000	27,000
Other	101,555	86,662	148,029	78,000	86,000
Total Export	214,000	171,523	231,779	150,000	151,000
Seed	13,893	15,018	11,737	10,372	13,034
Domestic	96,603	53,467	53,994	48,980	45,000
Total Usage	324,496	240,007	297,510	209,352	209,034
Ending Stock	86,000	69,000	21,000	48,000	32,000
Stocks/Use	26.5 %	28.7 %	7.1 %	22.9 %	15.3 %

Forecasts by STAT Market Research based on USDA and U.S. Department of Commerce data

Australian Lentil Supply and Demand Estimates

(metric tons, acres)

Year	2010	2011	2012	2013	2014
Acreage	408,951	426,989	406,232	416,116	395,360
Yield (lbs)	1,651	1,585	1,484	1,340	1,472
Production	306,210	307,000	273,500	253,000	264,000
Carry In	97,000	143,000	55,000	16,000	17,000
Imports	1,170	1,029	1,000	1,200	1,100
Stocks	404,381	451,029	329,500	270,200	282,100
Disappearance					
Nov-Apr Exports	102,647	148,622	147,614	194,445	N/A
% of Annual	41.6 %	38.9 %	49.3 %	81.0 %	N/A
Export	246,666	382,171	299,627	240,000	248,000
Seed, Feed, Waste	14,715	13,858	13,873	13,200	14,100
Total Usage	261,381	396,029	313,500	253,200	262,100
Ending Stock	143,000	55,000	16,000	17,000	20,000
Stocks/Use	54.7 %	13.9 %	5.1 %	6.7 %	7.6 %

Forecasts by STAT Market Research based on data from ABARE, ABS and Pulse Australia

Canadian All Lentil Exports April, 2014
(metric tons)

Crop Year	2011-12	2012-13	2012-13	2013-14	2014
Period	Aug-Jul	Aug-Jul	Aug-Apr	Aug-Apr	Apr
Top Five Buyers					
India	169,504	625,231	398,958	271,720	32,008
Turkey	206,308	169,371	136,623	259,994	19,342
Egypt	64,905	53,550	51,353	83,273	3,464
United Arab Emirates	83,656	110,658	64,504	82,438	8,620
Algeria	63,564	80,982	72,212	55,525	2,377
Subtotal	587,937	1,039,792	723,649	752,951	65,810
Percent of Total	51.2%	63.4%	64.0%	61.8%	53.0%
All Buyers					
United States	27,480	22,706	18,209	17,666	2,705
Total N. America	27,480	22,706	18,209	17,666	2,705
Austria	68	0	0	22	0
Belgium	3,810	3,410	2,444	4,878	981
Denmark	25	26	0	0	0
France	6,570	10,268	8,629	7,266	835
Germany	11,458	10,907	8,394	10,459	1,328
Greece	10,024	9,145	8,786	6,869	370
Iceland	193	324	50	0	0
Ireland	86	0	0	45	0
Italy	22,652	16,595	12,893	17,941	1,516
Netherlands	2,691	2,151	1,289	6,448	1,911
Portugal	709	1,948	930	924	96
Spain	40,487	58,141	44,619	38,107	4,215
Sweden	307	260	168	345	90
Switzerland	327	36	25	244	45
United Kingdom	11,196	9,401	7,403	8,893	1,078
Total W. Europe	110,602	122,612	95,630	102,440	12,465

Canadian All Lentil Exports April, 2014

(metric tons)

Crop Year	2011-12	2012-13	2012-13	2013-14	2014
Period	Aug-Jul	Aug-Jul	Aug-Apr	Aug-Apr	Apr
Albania	47	74	49	200	0
Armenia	233	264	139	366	73
Bosnia and Herzegovina	49	65	65	25	0
Bulgaria	3,356	3,930	3,223	4,386	193
Croatia	289	261	182	374	47
Czech Republic	2,060	1,963	1,183	1,729	25
Georgia	189	463	371	723	75
Hungary	1,402	610	498	887	0
Lithuania	0	21	21	0	0
Macedonia	207	0	0	176	0
Poland	547	769	580	847	145
Romania	43	22	0	22	0
Russia	652	702	554	391	96
Serbia	86	43	43	50	0
Slovakia	86	124	124	201	0
Slovenia	0	103	103	0	0
Ukraine	45	147	72	68	0
Uzbekistan	0	474	474	0	0
Total E. Europe	9,293	10,035	7,683	10,446	655
Bahrain	170	74	74	100	0
Cyprus	1,012	995	873	764	43
Egypt	64,905	53,550	51,353	83,273	3,464
Iran	5,550	943	271	0	0
Israel	5,284	5,180	4,731	9,105	621
Jordan	1,823	2,688	2,564	3,915	382
Kuwait	243	138	112	56	0
Lebanon	6,334	5,945	4,555	4,814	649
Libya	100	200	147	206	0
Qatar	853	175	175	0	0
Saudi Arabia	4,811	6,707	6,315	7,104	196
Sudan	500	0	0	1,510	0
Syria	549	0	0	0	0
Turkey	206,308	169,371	136,623	259,994	19,342
United Arab Emirates	83,656	110,658	64,504	82,438	8,620
Yemen	2,113	1,032	574	1,060	509
Total Middle East	384,211	357,656	272,870	454,341	33,827

Canadian All Lentil Exports April, 2014
(metric tons)

Crop Year	2011-12	2012-13	2012-13	2013-14	2014
Period	Aug-Jul	Aug-Jul	Aug-Apr	Aug-Apr	Apr
Algeria	63,564	80,982	72,212	55,525	2,377
Cape Verde	0	100	75	125	0
Comoros	0	70	0	0	0
Cote D'ivoire	0	0	0	12	0
Djibouti	25	0	0	0	0
Equatorial Guinea	0	4	0	0	0
Gabon	0	0	0	27	0
Kenya	699	174	174	250	0
Mauritania	195	979	979	0	0
Mauritius	692	1,325	1,149	1,112	99
Morocco	3,968	7,054	5,755	5,296	1,336
Saint Helena	0	79	79	0	0
Senegal	125	170	95	25	0
South Africa	5,395	4,052	3,467	3,838	925
Tunisia	1,278	730	704	2,145	0
Total Africa	75,941	95,720	84,689	68,356	4,737
Bangladesh	47,627	90,800	56,056	35,939	1,649
Cambodia	180	0	0	22	0
China	191	3,782	3,702	20,639	0
Hong Kong	291	200	9	0	0
India	169,504	625,231	398,958	271,720	32,008
Indonesia	190	1,159	1,159	55	0
Japan	397	250	18	136	21
Korea South	120	43	0	72	0
Malaysia	4,887	157	114	150	25
Myanmar	0	0	0	368	0
Nepal	1,011	3,199	2,186	3,301	1,302
Pakistan	68,527	31,041	15,497	37,594	4,434
Philippines	343	371	215	370	157
Singapore	283	3,084	2,021	261	25
Sri Lanka	14,715	50,587	26,974	37,845	7,270
Taiwan	108	22	22	4	0
Thailand	170	0	0	0	0
Vietnam	0	249	0	0	0
Total Asia	308,543	810,177	506,931	408,475	46,891
Australia	1,029	1,028	717	738	219
Cocos Islands	0	0	0	263	0
New Zealand	168	162	82	143	15
Papua New Guinea	0	0	0	50	0
Total Pacific	1,197	1,190	799	1,194	234

Canadian All Lentil Exports April, 2014

(metric tons)

Crop Year	2011-12	2012-13	2012-13	2013-14	2014
Period	Aug-Jul	Aug-Jul	Aug-Apr	Aug-Apr	Apr
Argentina	0	1,413	1,216	809	394
Bolivia	535	1,242	771	786	25
Brazil	11,217	16,283	10,054	11,007	736
Chile	15,956	16,260	9,128	10,000	1,149
Colombia	65,226	64,345	41,578	33,473	7,860
Ecuador	15,513	21,377	15,152	8,603	1,914
Paraguay	90	47	22	50	0
Peru	30,172	27,828	18,450	20,714	2,692
Suriname	0	0	0	28	0
Uruguay	1,568	3,113	1,808	2,738	1,046
Venezuela	40,609	26,785	14,673	28,787	2,721
Total S. America	180,886	178,692	112,851	116,994	18,536
Antigua and Barbuda	5	20	14	14	5
Aruba	2	1	1	1	0
Barbados	20	20	20	16	0
Costa Rica	669	860	628	533	100
Cuba	0	5	4	0	0
Dominica	118	188	147	134	11
Dominican Republic	460	642	561	383	74
Grenada	86	109	78	40	1
Guatemala	128	148	77	168	0
Jamaica	2	117	26	68	0
Mexico	40,264	28,952	23,669	30,215	3,239
Panama	6,152	7,201	4,743	4,947	463
Saint Kitts and Nevis	1	0	0	0	0
Saint Lucia	49	34	27	7	0
Saint Vincent and the Grenadines	73	65	63	80	0
Trinidad	1,824	1,898	1,074	1,074	236
Total C. America	49,851	40,259	31,132	37,679	4,129
Total World	1,148,004	1,639,046	1,130,795	1,217,590	124,180

Source: Statistics Canada

U.S. Lentil Exports April, 2014
(metric tons)

Crop Year	2011-12	2012-13	2012-13	2013-14	2014
Period	Sep-Aug	Sep-Aug	Sep-Apr	Sep-Apr	Apr
Top Five Buyers					
India	23,308	82,839	62,681	27,429	7,796
Spain	20,681	31,275	24,614	23,201	2,197
Italy	11,604	7,634	5,552	5,789	212
Kenya	0	1,814	1,714	5,649	0
Mexico	4,693	20,275	12,342	5,489	1,416
Subtotal	60,286	143,837	106,902	67,558	11,622
Percent of Total	35.1%	62.1%	60.8%	63.9%	61.4%
All Buyers					
Canada	12,493	9,015	6,775	4,856	1,114
Total N. America	12,493	9,015	6,775	4,856	1,114
Belgium	5,349	1,024	698	1,128	0
France	168	1,160	733	255	57
Germany	8,771	2,613	2,346	281	0
Greece	1,656	2,074	1,935	1,569	207
Italy	11,604	7,634	5,552	5,789	212
Netherlands	1,164	1,173	1,031	150	23
Norway	0	1	0	0	0
Portugal	0	0	0	834	139
Spain	20,681	31,275	24,614	23,201	2,197
United Kingdom	124	226	226	0	0
Total W. Europe	49,516	47,179	37,134	33,207	2,836
Georgia	3,607	0	0	0	0
Poland	47	0	0	0	0
Russia	471	365	151	475	22
Total E. Europe	4,125	365	151	475	22
Cyprus	25	47	47	23	0
Egypt	973	2,948	2,857	2,345	1,657
Ethiopia	369	8,131	8,131	0	0
Iran	0	15,357	15,357	0	0
Israel	1,873	2	2	105	21
Jordan	1,967	0	0	47	0
Lebanon	83	47	47	0	0
Saudi Arabia	186	448	448	364	0
Somalia	1,875	0	0	0	0
Sudan	26,750	4,811	4,215	0	0
Syria	2,800	0	0	0	0
Turkey	4,771	3,127	2,920	927	152
United Arab Emirates	728	1,258	23	4,200	807
Total Middle East	42,400	36,176	34,047	8,012	2,637

U.S. Lentil Exports April, 2014

(metric tons)

Crop Year	2011-12	2012-13	2012-13	2013-14	2014
Period	Sep-Aug	Sep-Aug	Sep-Apr	Sep-Apr	Apr
Algeria	665	1,554	1,554	702	0
Benin	0	393	323	0	0
Burkina Faso	806	499	319	190	0
Cameroon	0	2,440	2,440	2,899	0
Chad	499	0	0	0	0
Djibouti	6,027	5,239	2,848	1,500	0
French Southern Territories	120	50	0	274	22
Kenya	0	1,814	1,714	5,649	0
Liberia	0	240	240	50	0
Mali	609	0	0	0	0
Mauritania	160	0	0	0	0
Morocco	0	281	281	71	71
Niger	400	53	53	2,100	1,310
Senegal	0	105	105	0	0
Sierra Leone	468	738	738	200	0
South Africa	25	0	0	0	0
Tanzania	0	0	0	271	0
Togo	0	0	0	50	50
Uganda	280	0	0	250	0
Total Africa	10,058	13,405	10,614	14,205	1,453
Bangladesh	2,071	1,394	746	478	0
Cambodia	0	70	70	0	0
China	317	86	86	0	0
Hong Kong	157	107	67	18	5
India	23,308	82,839	62,681	27,429	7,796
Indonesia	180	114	114	0	0
Japan	279	334	186	288	0
Korea South	0	10	5	63	0
Laos	0	148	0	0	0
Nepal	0	261	0	0	0
Pakistan	2,843	1,722	542	732	90
Philippines	11	6	6	6	0
Sri Lanka	732	2,221	1,672	352	0
Taiwan	11	50	44	0	0
Thailand	3	0	0	0	0

U.S. Lentil Exports April, 2014
(metric tons)

Crop Year	2011-12	2012-13	2012-13	2013-14	2014
Period	Sep-Aug	Sep-Aug	Sep-Apr	Sep-Apr	Apr
Total Asia	29,912	89,362	66,217	29,367	7,891
Australia	0	16	16	0	0
French Polynesia	1,253	1,747	1,345	1,108	199
New Zealand	3	0	0	2	0
Total Pacific	1,256	1,762	1,361	1,110	199
Brazil	3	0	0	0	0
Chile	230	100	0	5	0
Colombia	876	784	65	2,426	216
Ecuador	212	0	0	20	0
Peru	13,839	11,514	6,062	5,393	1,011
Venezuela	142	0	0	0	0
Total S. America	15,301	12,398	6,127	7,845	1,227
Barbados	104	125	91	53	0
Costa Rica	328	7	7	0	0
Dominican Republic	88	111	81	100	3
El Salvador	0	1	0	0	0
Guatemala	38	0	0	93	0
Haiti	943	607	607	0	0
Honduras	9	4	4	11	3
Jamaica	39	17	14	7	0
Leeward Windward Is.	61	925	370	839	136
Mexico	4,693	20,275	12,342	5,489	1,416
Netherlands Antilles	20	34	16	16	4
Nicaragua	2	4	2	49	0
Panama	3	7	0	0	0
Trinidad	137	0	0	0	0
Total C. America	6,463	22,117	13,533	6,656	1,563
Total World	171,524	231,780	175,959	105,732	18,940

Source: U.S. Department of Commerce

Australian Lentil Exports April, 2014

(metric tons)

Crop Year	2011-12	2012-13	2012-13	2013-14	2014
Period	Nov-Oct	Nov-Oct	Nov-Apr	Nov-Apr	Apr
Top Five Buyers					
Bangladesh	93,954	84,676	40,206	56,376	3,802
India	58,049	62,145	25,978	50,720	17,194
Sri Lanka	99,540	88,209	46,730	40,076	7,322
Pakistan	32,745	16,268	5,300	17,324	2,620
United Arab Emirates	58,597	32,316	20,428	15,775	1,638
Subtotal	342,885	283,614	138,643	180,272	32,577
Percent of Total	89.8%	94.7%	93.9%	92.7%	96.3%
All Buyers					
Canada	250	0	0	0	0
United States	0	0	0	24	0
Total N. America	250	0	0	24	0
Belgium	96	0	0	0	0
France	72	0	0	0	0
Italy	212	24	24	48	24
Spain	120	97	97	0	0
United Kingdom	317	289	98	126	53
Total W. Europe	817	410	219	174	77
Ukraine	0	0	0	140	0
Total E. Europe	0	0	0	140	0
Egypt	26,464	7,598	4,182	6,752	626
Israel	74	25	0	96	0
Lebanon	1,225	1,078	574	722	50
Saudi Arabia	0	307	235	0	0
Sudan	0	1,008	1,008	0	0
Turkey	3,912	0	0	2,803	0
United Arab Emirates	58,597	32,316	20,428	15,775	1,638
Yemen	1,406	1,231	836	1,104	147
Total Middle East	91,677	43,564	27,264	27,252	2,461
Kenya	125	0	0	0	0
Mauritius	2,433	1,272	735	705	101
Morocco	197	0	0	0	0
Reunion	0	125	25	0	0
South Africa	1,017	1,597	617	781	198
Total Africa	3,772	2,995	1,377	1,486	299
Bangladesh	93,954	84,676	40,206	56,376	3,802

Australian Lentil Exports April, 2014
(metric tons)

Crop Year	2011-12	2012-13	2012-13	2013-14	2014
Period	Nov-Oct	Nov-Oct	Nov-Apr	Nov-Apr	Apr
India	58,049	62,145	25,978	50,720	17,194
Japan	39	21	0	23	0
Korea South	43	0	0	18	18
Malaysia	122	0	0	0	0
Nepal	435	909	295	613	0
Pakistan	32,745	16,268	5,300	17,324	2,620
Singapore	117	48	0	48	0
Sri Lanka	99,540	88,209	46,730	40,076	7,322
Taiwan	143	187	163	96	24
Thailand	48	45	28	2	0
Vietnam	0	24	0	0	0
Total Asia	285,233	252,533	118,701	165,296	30,980
Fiji	22	24	0	0	0
New Zealand	55	100	52	72	0
Papua New Guinea	77	1	1	0	0
Total Pacific	154	125	53	72	0
Netherlands Antilles	25	0	0	0	0
Total C. America	25	0	0	0	0
Total World	381,927	299,627	147,614	194,445	33,818

Source: Australia Bureau of Statistics

Red Lentils

Canadian Red Lentil Supply and Demand Estimates
(metric tons, acres)

Year	2010	2011	2012	2013	2014
Area (acres)	1,920,000	1,227,800	950,000	1,217,000	1,831,000
Yield (lbs)	1,263	1,418	1,362	1,853	1,439
Production	1,100,200	789,800	586,700	1,022,800	1,195,000
Carry In	11,000	489,000	518,000	25,000	21,000
Stocks	1,111,200	1,278,800	1,104,700	1,047,800	1,216,000
Disappearance					
Export	572,631	581,584	889,905	843,600	971,300
Seed	37,300	29,500	37,800	56,900	48,000
Feed & Waste	12,269	149,716	151,995	126,300	91,700
Total Usage	622,200	760,800	1,079,700	1,026,800	1,111,000
Ending Stock	489,000	518,000	25,000	21,000	105,000
Stocks/Use	78.6%	68.1%	2.3%	2.0%	9.5%

Forecasts by STAT Market Research based on data from Statistics Canada

Canadian Red Lentil Exports April, 2014
(metric tons)

Crop Year	2011-12	2012-13	2012-13	2013-14	2014
Period	Aug-Jul	Aug-Jul	Aug-Apr	Aug-Apr	Apr
Top Five Buyers					
Turkey	173,771	131,831	108,110	223,259	17,108
India	148,696	468,723	318,517	202,951	17,585
Egypt	52,300	46,399	45,019	74,035	2,658
Sri Lanka	13,862	48,502	26,042	36,493	6,722
Pakistan	65,775	29,842	15,219	34,630	3,973
Subtotal	454,405	725,298	512,906	571,368	48,045
Percent of Total	81.4%	81.5%	82.6%	81.9%	83.0%
All Buyers					
United States	13,575	4,656	3,646	3,080	513
Total N. America	13,575	4,656	3,646	3,080	513
Belgium	69	158	71	428	207
France	336	743	700	678	77
Germany	291	601	163	853	100
Greece	92	175	175	358	0
Iceland	193	274	0	0	0
Ireland	0	0	0	45	0
Italy	4,265	2,667	2,205	2,922	166
Netherlands	0	170	119	1,113	1,011
Portugal	375	616	250	373	0
Spain	2,136	1,980	1,839	1,124	49
Sweden	25	21	0	0	0
Switzerland	25	0	0	0	0
United Kingdom	7,833	5,783	4,747	6,459	638
Total W. Europe	15,640	13,188	10,268	14,354	2,247
Armenia	0	0	0	17	0
Bulgaria	170	22	0	0	0
Croatia	56	0	0	12	0
Czech Republic	2	23	23	11	0
Georgia	5	0	0	0	0
Poland	112	153	129	331	74
Romania	0	11	0	11	0
Russia	49	22	22	50	0
Ukraine	35	147	72	68	0
Total E. Europe	429	378	246	499	74

Canadian Red Lentil Exports April, 2014

(metric tons)

Crop Year	2011-12	2012-13	2012-13	2013-14	2014
Period	Aug-Jul	Aug-Jul	Aug-Apr	Aug-Apr	Apr
Bahrain	96	0	0	25	0
Cyprus	36	6	6	19	0
Egypt	52,300	46,399	45,019	74,035	2,658
Iran	0	1	1	0	0
Israel	929	1,048	926	3,554	98
Jordan	413	275	275	1,153	75
Kuwait	2	54	28	3	0
Lebanon	115	350	350	363	75
Qatar	853	125	125	0	0
Saudi Arabia	3,375	3,870	3,652	6,044	55
Sudan	500	0	0	1,510	0
Turkey	173,771	131,831	108,110	223,259	17,108
United Arab Emirates	6,774	37,911	23,855	32,724	2,939
Yemen	912	982	524	1,060	509
Total Middle East	240,074	222,853	182,871	343,748	23,517
Algeria	100	728	728	0	0
Djibouti	25	0	0	0	0
Kenya	699	124	124	250	0
Mauritania	102	46	46	0	0
Mauritius	280	543	433	525	0
Morocco	0	125	125	0	0
South Africa	2,026	1,193	909	1,065	374
Tunisia	1,011	302	275	1,465	0
Total Africa	4,243	3,060	2,640	3,304	374
Bangladesh	43,560	88,690	54,622	34,394	1,649
China	13	433	433	17,987	0
Hong Kong	13	2	2	0	0
India	148,696	468,723	318,517	202,951	17,585
Indonesia	190	948	948	55	0
Japan	137	150	0	47	21
Korea South	0	43	0	72	0
Malaysia	4,845	157	114	150	25
Myanmar	0	0	0	368	0
Nepal	1,011	2,927	2,186	2,470	1,028
Pakistan	65,775	29,842	15,219	34,630	3,973
Philippines	268	125	125	0	0
Singapore	283	2,615	1,798	261	25
Sri Lanka	13,862	48,502	26,042	36,493	6,722
Taiwan	18	22	22	0	0

Canadian Red Lentil Exports April, 2014

(metric tons)

Crop Year	2011-12	2012-13	2012-13	2013-14	2014
Period	Aug-Jul	Aug-Jul	Aug-Apr	Aug-Apr	Apr
Total Asia	278,671	643,180	420,028	329,876	31,028
Australia	28	12	4	20	0
New Zealand	86	51	51	64	0
Total Pacific	113	63	55	84	0
Argentina	0	9	0	0	0
Bolivia	182	0	0	0	0
Brazil	12	175	175	285	0
Chile	175	206	100	0	0
Colombia	1,019	442	392	1,423	0
Ecuador	72	0	0	0	0
Paraguay	23	0	0	0	0
Peru	576	54	54	586	125
Venezuela	0	648	0	184	0
Total S. America	2,059	1,535	721	2,478	125
Costa Rica	0	0	0	25	0
Guatemala	3	0	0	0	0
Jamaica	1	2	2	25	0
Mexico	3,038	901	361	89	0
Panama	76	33	26	26	5
Trinidad	61	57	4	34	0
Total C. America	3,179	993	394	199	5
Total World	557,984	889,905	620,868	697,622	57,882

Source: Statistics Canada

Green Lentils

Canadian Green Lentil Exports April, 2014
(metric tons)

Crop Year	2011-12	2012-13	2012-13	2013-14	2014
Period	Aug-Jul	Aug-Jul	Aug-Apr	Aug-Apr	Apr
Top Five Buyers					
India	19,650	155,716	79,953	68,307	14,423
Algeria	61,466	78,207	69,436	55,525	2,377
United Arab Emirates	73,859	72,747	40,649	49,711	5,682
Turkey	22,888	37,263	28,513	36,600	2,234
Spain	36,903	56,161	42,781	34,005	3,867
Subtotal	214,766	400,094	261,332	244,148	28,583
Percent of Total	39.7%	55.1%	53.2%	48.8%	44.5%
All Buyers					
United States	5,109	4,375	3,397	7,190	1,373
Total N. America	5,109	4,375	3,397	7,190	1,373
Austria	68	0	0	22	0
Belgium	3,698	3,180	2,321	3,719	733
Denmark	25	26	0	0	0
France	6,148	9,433	7,838	6,512	715
Germany	9,917	10,019	7,944	9,020	1,124
Greece	9,751	8,280	7,920	6,489	370
Iceland	0	50	50	0	0
Ireland	86	0	0	0	0
Italy	18,233	13,813	10,573	14,850	1,329
Netherlands	2,406	1,851	1,086	4,638	882
Portugal	310	1,332	681	448	96
Spain	36,903	56,161	42,781	34,005	3,867
Sweden	282	213	142	323	90
Switzerland	302	36	25	244	45
United Kingdom	3,341	3,593	2,655	2,285	382
Total W. Europe	91,470	107,986	84,015	82,555	9,634

Canadian Green Lentil Exports April, 2014
(metric tons)

Crop Year Period	2011-12 Aug-Jul	2012-13 Aug-Jul	2012-13 Aug-Apr	2013-14 Aug-Apr	2014 Apr
Albania	47	74	49	200	0
Armenia	233	264	139	349	73
Bosnia and Herzegovina	49	65	65	25	0
Bulgaria	3,186	3,908	3,223	4,386	193
Croatia	234	261	182	362	47
Czech Republic	2,032	1,941	1,161	1,719	25
Georgia	184	463	371	723	75
Hungary	1,359	610	498	887	0
Lithuania	0	21	21	0	0
Macedonia	207	0	0	176	0
Poland	299	588	446	510	71
Romania	43	11	0	11	0
Russia	537	681	533	341	96
Slovakia	86	124	124	201	0
Slovenia	0	103	103	0	0
Ukraine	10	0	0	0	0
Uzbekistan	0	474	474	0	0
Yugoslavia	86	43	43	50	0
Total E. Europe	8,593	9,629	7,432	9,940	581
Bahrain	50	74	74	75	0
Cyprus	976	989	867	745	43
Egypt	11,187	7,151	6,334	9,239	806
Iran	5,550	942	270	0	0
Israel	4,280	4,057	3,780	5,413	523
Jordan	1,411	2,363	2,239	2,763	307
Kuwait	241	81	81	0	0
Lebanon	6,023	5,595	4,205	4,452	574
Libya	100	200	147	206	0
Qatar	0	50	50	0	0
Saudi Arabia	1,436	2,686	2,512	912	141
Syria	549	0	0	0	0
Turkey	22,888	37,263	28,513	36,600	2,234
United Arab Emirates	73,859	72,747	40,649	49,711	5,682
Yemen	1,201	50	50	0	0
Total Middle East	129,751	134,247	89,770	110,114	10,311

Canadian Green Lentil Exports April, 2014

(metric tons)

Crop Year Period	2011-12 Aug-Jul	2012-13 Aug-Jul	2012-13 Aug-Apr	2013-14 Aug-Apr	2014 Apr
Algeria	61,466	78,207	69,436	55,525	2,377
Cape Verde	0	100	75	125	0
Comoros	0	70	0	0	0
Cote D'ivoire	0	0	0	12	0
Equatorial Guinea	0	4	0	0	0
Gabon	0	0	0	27	0
Kenya	0	50	50	0	0
Mauritania	93	78	78	0	0
Mauritius	412	783	717	557	99
Morocco	3,706	6,857	5,558	5,296	1,336
Saint Helena	0	79	79	0	0
Senegal	125	170	95	25	0
South Africa	3,344	2,859	2,557	2,773	551
Tunisia	267	229	229	681	0
Total Africa	69,413	89,486	78,875	65,021	4,363
Bangladesh	3,928	2,110	1,434	1,243	0
Cambodia	0	0	0	22	0
China	178	3,349	3,269	2,440	0
Hong Kong	249	189	0	0	0
India	19,650	155,716	79,953	68,307	14,423
Indonesia	0	211	211	0	0
Japan	238	100	18	39	0
Korea South	120	0	0	0	0
Malaysia	42	0	0	0	0
Nepal	0	273	0	831	274
Pakistan	2,242	1,198	279	2,857	436
Philippines	75	246	89	238	157
Singapore	0	468	221	0	0
Sri Lanka	853	1,775	673	1,277	548
Taiwan	90	0	0	0	0
Thailand	170	0	0	0	0
Vietnam	0	249	0	0	0
Total Asia	27,837	165,885	86,148	77,253	15,839
Australia	920	928	633	673	219
New Zealand	83	103	23	79	15
Papua New Guinea	0	0	0	50	0
Total Pacific	1,002	1,031	656	802	234

Canadian Green Lentil Exports April, 2014

(metric tons)

Crop Year	2011-12	2012-13	2012-13	2013-14	2014
Period	Aug-Jul	Aug-Jul	Aug-Apr	Aug-Apr	Apr
Argentina	0	1,351	1,189	730	394
Bolivia	353	1,242	771	786	25
Brazil	11,005	16,058	9,879	10,172	736
Chile	14,841	16,029	9,028	9,907	1,118
Colombia	56,282	63,458	40,820	31,549	7,829
Ecuador	14,266	20,904	15,046	8,295	1,914
Paraguay	67	47	22	50	0
Peru	27,200	27,616	18,344	19,812	2,461
Suriname	0	0	0	2	0
Uruguay	1,493	3,113	1,808	2,738	1,046
Venezuela	37,029	26,061	14,673	28,603	2,721
Total S. America	162,537	175,879	111,581	112,644	18,244
Antigua and Barbuda	5	20	14	14	5
Aruba	2	1	1	1	0
Barbados	20	20	20	16	0
Costa Rica	669	860	628	508	100
Cuba	0	5	4	0	0
Dominica	118	188	147	134	11
Dominican Republic	460	642	561	358	74
Grenada	86	109	78	40	1
Guatemala	125	148	77	97	0
Jamaica	1	74	24	0	0
Mexico	35,920	26,226	21,574	27,399	2,775
Panama	5,827	7,046	4,692	4,745	458
Saint Kitts and Nevis	1	0	0	0	0
Saint Lucia	49	34	27	7	0
Saint Vincent and the Grenadines	73	65	63	80	0
Trinidad	1,763	1,760	1,044	922	210
Total C. America	45,118	37,197	28,953	34,320	3,634
Total World	540,828	725,716	490,827	499,840	64,214

Source: Statistics Canada

Peas

World Pea Supply and Demand Situation

(hectares, metric tons, kilograms)

	2010	2011	2012	2013	2014
Area (hectares)	6,620,000	6,170,000	6,810,000	6,990,000	7,380,000
Yield (kg/ha)	1,567	1,622	1,536	1,590	1,579
Production	10,374,000	10,010,000	10,458,000	11,117,000	11,650,000
Carry-in	1,250,000	990,000	550,000	410,000	740,000
Supply	11,624,000	11,000,000	11,008,000	11,527,000	12,390,000
Trade	4,480,000	3,150,000	3,800,000	4,340,000	4,560,000
Inferred Use	10,634,000	10,450,000	10,598,000	10,787,000	11,290,000
Ending Stock	990,000	550,000	410,000	740,000	1,100,000
Stock-Use Ratio	9.3%	5.3%	3.9%	6.9%	9.7%
Per Capita Use (kg)	1.552	1.508	1.513	1.524	1.595

Estimates by STAT Publishing based data from the FAO, USDA, Statistics Canada, ABARES, and other entities.

Field Pea Production Summary in Selected Countries

(hectares, metric tons, kilograms)

Area (hectares)	2010	2011	2012	2013	2014
Australia	296,000	249,000	281,000	245,000	245,000
Canada	1,467,000	986,000	1,510,000	1,329,000	1,609,000
United States	306,000	146,000	263,000	348,000	373,000
France	240,000	183,000	134,000	119,000	122,000
Russia	820,000	1,141,000	1,160,000	1,547,000	1,623,000
Ukraine	279,000	245,000	222,000	244,000	220,000
Indian Subcont.	861,000	824,000	837,000	832,000	830,000
Other	2,350,000	2,393,000	2,400,000	2,329,000	2,360,000
Total	6,619,000	6,167,000	6,807,000	6,993,000	7,382,000
Production (MT)	2010	2011	2012	2013	2014
Australia	428,000	342,000	319,000	342,000	334,000
Canada	3,018,000	2,502,000	3,341,000	3,849,000	3,835,000
United States	645,000	255,000	493,000	709,000	730,000
France	1,096,000	676,000	553,000	488,000	526,000
Russia	1,188,000	2,021,000	1,660,000	1,684,000	2,197,000
Ukraine	452,000	364,000	351,000	403,000	354,000
Indian Subcont.	741,000	664,000	777,000	749,000	728,000
Other	2,806,000	3,186,000	2,964,000	2,893,000	2,946,000
Total	10,374,000	10,010,000	10,458,000	11,117,000	11,650,000
Yields (kg per hectare)	2010	2011	2012	2013	2014
Australia	1,446	1,373	1,135	1,396	1,363
Canada	2,057	2,538	2,213	2,896	2,383
United States	2,108	1,747	1,875	2,037	1,957
France	4,567	3,694	4,127	4,101	4,311
Russia	1,449	1,771	1,431	1,089	1,354
Ukraine	1,620	1,486	1,581	1,652	1,609
Indian Subcont.	861	806	928	900	877
Other	1,194	1,331	1,235	1,242	1,248
World Yield	1,567	1,623	1,536	1,590	1,578

Projections by STAT Market Research based on data from Statistics Canada, ABARE, UNIP, USDA, FAO

Canadian Field Pea Supply and Demand Estimates

(metric tons, acres)

Year	2010	2011	2012	2013	2014
Area (acres)	3,625,000	2,436,700	3,730,000	3,285,000	3,975,000
Yield (lbs)	1,836	2,264	1,974	2,583	2,127
Production	3,018,200	2,502,000	3,340,500	3,849,300	3,835,000
Carry In	910,000	535,000	295,000	174,000	450,000
Imports	42,814	13,204	18,848	25,000	25,300
Stocks	3,971,015	3,050,204	3,654,348	4,048,300	4,310,300
Disappearance					
Aug-Apr Exports	2,488,488	1,764,468	2,024,983	1,957,135	N/A
Percent of Forecast	82.5 %	84.1 %	76.3 %	77.3 %	N/A
Europe	128,017	23,854	117,421	50,400	63,000
South America	76,168	84,589	66,484	71,100	75,000
N/C America	121,260	138,571	159,576	206,300	177,000
Pacific Rim	2,588,812	1,807,488	2,253,833	2,113,900	2,264,000
Arab/Africa	100,903	44,358	57,201	90,600	67,000
Export	3,015,159	2,098,859	2,654,515	2,532,300	2,646,000
Seed	171,000	262,000	231,000	279,000	216,000
Feed & Waste	174,856	319,344	533,886	709,700	563,300
Domestic	75,000	75,000	60,948	77,300	75,000
Total Usage	3,436,015	2,755,204	3,480,348	3,598,300	3,500,300
Ending Stock	535,000	295,000	174,000	450,000	810,000
Stocks/Use	15.6 %	10.7 %	5.0 %	12.5 %	23.1 %

Forecasts by STAT Market Research based on data from Statistics Canada

Ukraine – Field Pea Supply and Demand Forecast

(hectares, metric tons)

	2009	2010	2011	2012	2013
Area (hectares)	273,000	278,500	244,900	295,000	284,000
Yield (kg/ha)	1,808	1,624	1,488	1,500	1,740
Production	493,600	452,400	364,300	443,000	494,000
Opening Stocks	10,000	42,600	42,000	32,000	17,000
Imports	380	448	426	400	400
Supply	503,980	495,448	406,726	475,400	511,400
Disappearance					
Exports	265,684	101,895	160,000	169,000	189,000
Domestic	195,696	351,553	214,726	289,400	286,400
Total Usage	461,380	453,448	374,726	458,400	475,400
Ending Stocks	42,600	42,000	32,000	17,000	36,000
Stocks/Use	9.2 %	9.3 %	8.5 %	3.7 %	7.6 %

Projections by STAT Market Research based on USDA and FAO data

U.S. Field Pea Supply and Demand Estimates

(metric tons, acres)

Year	2010	2011	2012	2013	2014
Acreage	756,000	362,000	649,000	860,000	921,000
Yield (lbs)	1,881	1,554	1,675	1,816	1,747
Production	645,060	255,148	493,151	708,519	730,000
Carryin	85,000	160,000	29,000	20,000	130,000
Stocks	730,060	415,148	522,151	728,519	860,000
Export and Domestic Usage					
Jul-Apr Exports	406,683	216,478	343,992	369,919	N/A
Percent of Forecast	90.0 %	82.9 %	89.6 %	87.5 %	N/A
Green Peas	124,649	101,531	121,267	157,000	163,000
Yellow Peas	124,781	25,818	128,953	125,000	137,000
Peas NES	113,812	55,470	47,061	67,000	139,000
Split Peas	88,581	78,388	86,542	74,000	99,000
Total Exports	451,822	261,207	383,823	423,000	538,000
Domestic	39,300	39,586	31,000	47,566	53,000
Net Seed	30,200	54,200	71,800	76,900	67,500
Feed & Waste	48,738	31,155	15,527	51,053	51,500
Total Usage	570,060	386,148	502,151	598,519	710,000
Ending Stocks	160,000	29,000	20,000	130,000	150,000
Stocks/Use Ratio	28.1 %	7.5 %	4.0 %	21.7 %	21.1 %

Forecasts by STAT Market Research based on USDA and U.S. Department of Commerce data

France – Field Pea Supply and Demand Estimates

(hectares, metric tons)

	2010-11	2011-12	2012-13	2013-14	2014-15
Area (ha)	240,000	183,000	134,000	119,000	122,000
Yield (kg/ha)	4,568	3,694	4,127	4,101	4,311
Production (MT)	1,096,300	676,000	553,000	488,000	526,000
Imports	10,853	12,000	11,000	12,000	10,000
Carryin	27,100	84,800	63,000	67,000	19,000
Stocks	1,134,253	772,800	627,000	567,000	555,000
Disappearance					
Exports	354,025	348,690	198,305	231,000	199,000
Seed & Food	72,500	59,850	56,700	51,500	51,800
Domestic Feed	622,928	301,260	304,995	265,500	264,200
Total Usage	1,049,453	709,800	560,000	548,000	515,000
Ending Stocks	84,800	63,000	67,000	19,000	40,000
Stocks to Use	8.1%	8.9%	12.0%	3.5%	7.8%

Projections by STAT Market Research based on information from UNIP and France Customs.

Australian Field Pea Supply and Demand Estimates
(metric tons, acres)

Year	2010	2011	2012	2013	2014
Acreage	731,045	615,279	693,116	605,395	605,395
Yield (lbs)	1,291	1,225	1,015	1,245	1,215
Production	427,940	342,000	319,000	342,000	333,600
Carry In	30,000	1,000	1,000	34,000	56,000
Stocks	457,940	343,000	320,000	376,000	389,600
Disappearance					
Nov-Apr Exports	141,173	68,613	98,767	86,348	N/A
% of Annual	48.3 %	33.5 %	59.0 %	53.3 %	N/A
Export	292,274	204,971	167,389	162,000	213,000
Seed	41,900	47,200	41,200	43,000	46,200
Feed & Other	122,766	89,829	77,411	115,000	109,300
Total Usage	456,940	342,000	286,000	320,000	368,500
Ending Stock	1,000	1,000	34,000	56,000	21,100
Stocks/Use	0.2 %	0.3 %	11.9 %	17.5 %	5.7 %

Forecasts by STAT Market Research based on data from ABARE, ABS and Pulse Australia

France – Field Pea Export Summary Mar 2014

(metric tons)

Crop Year	2011-12	2012-13	Jul-Mar	Jul-Mar	Mar
Period	Jul-Jun	Jul-Jun	2012	2013	2014
Belgium	59,315	67,390	48,755	66,700	4,710
Germany	13,850	27,925	15,865	10,970	6,310
Netherlands	23,625	21,735	12,795	12,720	1,990
Spain	8,555	7,745	6,520	6,980	101
Italy	6,933	7,367	6,361	8,548	186
Ireland	3	3	3		
United Kingdom	5,421	8,593	3,909	4,974	57
Switzerland	1,546	9,048	4,773	9,292	1,370
Norway	16,100	21,685	12,150	19,235	
India	204,093	23,275			
Egypt	7,554	1,956	1,956	5,683	1,100
Others	1,695	1,583	1,258	2,108	51
Total	348,690	198,305	114,345	147,210	15,875
Export Volume Split					
Europe	38.8 %	86.5 %	97.2 %	94.7 %	92.7 %
Other	61.2 %	13.5 %	2.8 %	5.3 %	7.3 %

BASED on data from French Customs and UNIP.

Green Peas

Canadian Green Pea Supply and Demand Estimates
(metric tons, acres)

Year	2010	2011	2012	2013	2014
Area (acres)	575,000	348,000	400,000	410,000	500,000
Yield (lbs)	1,764	2,039	2,188	2,847	2,213
Production	460,200	321,900	397,000	529,400	501,900
Carry In	99,000	106,000	31,000	11,000	89,800
Imports	11,800	3,700	5,300	6,800	6,900
Stocks	571,000	431,600	433,300	547,200	598,600
Disappearance					
Export	406,525	316,737	277,802	342,300	367,500
Seed	24,000	28,000	29,000	35,000	29,000
Feed & Waste	34,476	55,863	115,498	80,100	101,000
Total Usage	465,001	400,600	422,300	457,400	497,500
Ending Stock	106,000	31,000	11,000	89,800	101,100
Stocks/Use	22.8%	7.7%	2.6%	19.6%	20.3%

Forecasts by STAT Market Research based on data from Statistics Canada

Canadian Green Pea Exports April, 2014
(metric tons)

Crop Year	2011-12	2012-13	2012-13	2013-14	2014
Period	Aug-Jul	Aug-Jul	Aug-Apr	Aug-Apr	Apr
Top Five Buyers					
China	82,262	61,716	61,446	66,825	1,602
India	50,663	31,047	27,014	61,208	4,446
Colombia	23,749	12,675	10,907	11,727	1,916
Philippines	14,096	6,814	4,437	10,969	1,670
Venezuela	7,308	5,896	3,580	10,076	672
Subtotal	178,078	118,148	107,384	160,804	10,306
Percent of Total	74.8%	69.0%	69.4%	69.3%	63.4%
All Buyers					
United States	5,594	2,138	1,686	4,293	138
Total N. America	5,594	2,138	1,686	4,293	138
Belgium	23	1,452	1,427	4,655	239
Denmark	69	495	495	0	0
France	88	377	352	1,247	570
Germany	1,064	892	878	464	0
Greece	6	12	12	27	0
Iceland	0	22	0	47	0
Italy	810	1,741	1,741	1,563	0
Malta	185	21	21	69	23
Netherlands	177	266	266	605	0
Norway	0	0	0	25	0
Portugal	34	76	76	398	25
Spain	1,415	648	605	1,454	25
Sweden	0	22	0	0	0
Switzerland	0	131	131	0	0
United Kingdom	51	1,706	1,615	437	0
Total W. Europe	3,921	7,861	7,620	10,990	882
Armenia	24	0	0	25	0
Bulgaria	0	0	0	50	0
Croatia	18	0	0	0	0
Czech Republic	25	25	25	47	22
Georgia	42	4	4	0	0
Poland	0	0	0	274	0
Romania	0	0	0	158	0
Russia	671	1,694	1,694	1,129	0
Total E. Europe	781	1,723	1,723	1,683	22

Canadian Green Pea Exports April, 2014

(metric tons)

Crop Year	2011-12	2012-13	2012-13	2013-14	2014
Period	Aug-Jul	Aug-Jul	Aug-Apr	Aug-Apr	Apr
Bahrain	0	0	0	50	0
Egypt	1,631	1,941	1,941	5,841	1,113
Israel	288	108	108	1,156	50
Jordan	224	98	98	347	0
Kuwait	148	0	0	26	0
Lebanon	0	75	75	75	0
Libya	0	0	0	409	23
Saudi Arabia	3,624	2,614	2,614	2,213	263
Turkey	25	189	189	335	0
United Arab Emirates	7,014	4,186	3,280	8,923	1,040
Yemen	6,053	5,216	4,460	7,811	352
Total Middle East	19,009	14,427	12,766	27,185	2,840
Algeria	1,261	1,563	1,563	2,565	103
Burkina Faso	1	0	0	1	0
Gambia	0	0	0	125	0
Mauritania	150	0	0	0	0
Mauritius	102	10	10	75	0
Morocco	249	0	0	1,472	229
Senegal	238	1,707	1,422	2,639	0
South Africa	2,142	1,045	900	796	0
Tunisia	248	75	75	229	0
Total Africa	4,391	4,399	3,970	7,902	331
Bangladesh	101	100	0	0	0
Cambodia	664	316	316	317	45
China	82,262	61,716	61,446	66,825	1,602
Hong Kong	0	2	2	0	0
India	50,663	31,047	27,014	61,208	4,446
Indonesia	2,923	351	351	162	0
Japan	2,542	2,015	1,479	1,531	284
Korea South	111	0	0	0	0
Macau	0	0	0	90	0
Malaysia	132	48	48	301	47
Nepal	3,601	2,299	2,299	954	0
Pakistan	510	506	506	649	0
Philippines	14,096	6,814	4,437	10,969	1,670
Singapore	193	0	0	800	0
Sri Lanka	937	612	404	585	0
Taiwan	898	764	764	1,119	90
Thailand	654	1,025	793	86	0
Vietnam	0	21	21	452	0
Total Asia	160,286	107,636	99,881	146,047	8,184

Canadian Green Pea Exports April, 2014
(metric tons)

Crop Year	2011-12	2012-13	2012-13	2013-14	2014
Period	Aug-Jul	Aug-Jul	Aug-Apr	Aug-Apr	Apr
Australia	85	0	0	108	21
Fiji	639	127	127	327	25
New Zealand	0	0	0	100	0
U.S. Minor Outlying Islands	0	0	0	2	0
Total Pacific	724	127	127	537	46
Argentina	0	256	256	250	0
Brazil	2,136	8,156	6,787	3,359	474
Chile	3,148	2,344	2,118	3,240	485
Colombia	23,749	12,675	10,907	11,727	1,916
Ecuador	1,514	821	730	1,364	193
Guyana	150	0	0	0	0
Peru	3,874	1,539	1,459	2,047	0
Suriname	0	48	48	12	0
Uruguay	0	0	0	16	0
Venezuela	7,308	5,896	3,580	10,076	672
Total S. America	41,878	31,733	25,885	32,090	3,740
Barbados	1	1	1	1	0
Costa Rica	458	302	236	307	71
Dominica	1	0	0	0	0
Dominican Republic	98	51	51	191	0
Grenada	9	0	0	0	0
Haiti	0	550	550	0	0
Mexico	532	132	132	666	0
Panama	236	57	57	40	0
Saint Vincent and the Grenadines	1	0	0	0	0
Trinidad	26	25	25	28	0
Total C. America	1,363	1,118	1,052	1,232	71
Total World	237,947	171,164	154,710	231,961	16,256

Source: Statistics Canada

U.S. Green Pea Exports April, 2014

(metric tons)

Crop Year	2011-12	2012-13	2012-13	2013-14	2014
Period	Sep-Aug	Sep-Aug	Sep-Apr	Sep-Apr	Apr
Top Five Buyers					
India	54,156	43,755	36,521	45,088	3,214
China	9,310	24,191	20,637	35,066	1,146
Philippines	12,850	7,789	6,048	14,200	491
Canada	6,329	5,808	2,822	10,439	1,422
Saudi Arabia	0	2,638	1,531	3,195	236
Subtotal	82,645	84,181	67,559	107,989	6,509
Percent of Total	78.5%	76.4%	76.5%	80.2%	66.7%
All Buyers					
Canada	6,329	5,808	2,822	10,439	1,422
Total N. America	6,329	5,808	2,822	10,439	1,422
Belgium	0	187	0	3,001	774
Denmark	0	0	0	20	20
France	0	0	0	47	0
Germany	176	0	0	0	0
Italy	90	419	303	732	25
Netherlands	0	0	0	299	0
Norway	85	68	68	50	0
Spain	10	138	138	101	0
Sweden	0	0	0	22	0
United Kingdom	0	550	500	1,100	225
Total W. Europe	361	1,361	1,008	5,371	1,043
Poland	0	0	0	23	0
Russia	76	611	611	1,482	423
Total E. Europe	76	611	611	1,505	423
Bahrain	0	0	0	23	0
Cyprus	71	0	0	0	0
Egypt	189	79	0	934	0
Israel	141	93	70	826	46
Jordan	255	63	63	538	0
Lebanon	0	0	0	93	0
Saudi Arabia	0	2,638	1,531	3,195	236
Turkey	1,806	115	115	1,265	0
United Arab Emirates	250	318	47	225	0
Total Middle East	2,712	3,307	1,826	7,100	282
Kenya	1,890	3,547	2,902	0	0
Morocco	0	0	0	488	488
South Africa	72	1,192	921	2,594	224
Tanzania	910	769	418	0	0
Uganda	497	0	0	0	0
Total Africa	3,369	5,508	4,242	3,082	711

U.S. Green Pea Exports April, 2014

(metric tons)

Crop Year Period	2011-12 Sep-Aug	2012-13 Sep-Aug	2012-13 Sep-Apr	2013-14 Sep-Apr	2014 Apr
Bangladesh	282	0	0	46	0
China	9,310	24,191	20,637	35,066	1,146
Hong Kong	25	685	673	68	0
India	54,156	43,755	36,521	45,088	3,214
Indonesia	865	113	113	69	0
Japan	334	393	157	128	0
Korea South	4,841	3,098	2,913	2,409	88
Malaysia	1,076	445	374	256	0
Nepal	0	175	175	156	156
Pakistan	721	0	0	133	0
Philippines	12,850	7,789	6,048	14,200	491
Sri Lanka	489	71	71	212	0
Taiwan	1,209	1,220	1,220	2,503	23
Thailand	297	227	207	226	23
Vietnam	0	203	189	382	162
Total Asia	86,454	82,364	69,296	100,941	5,303
Australia	0	82	0	44	23
French Polynesia	3	0	0	40	0
South Georgia and the South Sandwich Islands	144	47	0	323	0
Total Pacific	147	129	0	406	23
Brazil	0	95	71	46	0
Chile	24	831	584	20	0
Colombia	1,377	4,282	4,027	2,281	253
Ecuador	0	280	280	69	0
Peru	1,710	997	497	1,902	47
Suriname	7	21	13	11	0
Total S. America	3,117	6,505	5,471	4,328	301

U.S. Green Pea Exports April, 2014

(metric tons)

Crop Year Period	2011-12 Sep-Aug	2012-13 Sep-Aug	2012-13 Sep-Apr	2013-14 Sep-Apr	2014 Apr
Barbados	0	0	0	3	3
Bermuda	7	0	0	0	0
Costa Rica	90	235	140	112	112
Dominican Republic	98	205	176	78	0
Guatemala	24	0	0	8	0
Haiti	498	20	20	0	0
Honduras	3	0	0	0	0
Jamaica	18	0	0	0	0
Leeward Windward Is.	119	0	0	0	0
Mexico	1,831	4,102	2,689	1,169	132
Panama	4	25	0	25	0
Trinidad	0	0	0	5	0
Total C. America	2,693	4,587	3,024	1,400	247
Total World	105,256	110,179	88,301	134,571	9,755

Source: U.S. Department of Commerce

Split and Whole Peas

Canadian Split Pea Exports April, 2014
(metric tons)

Crop Year	2011-12	2012-13	2012-13	2013-14	2014
Period	Aug-Jul	Aug-Jul	Aug-Apr	Aug-Apr	Apr
Top Five Buyers					
United States	12,695	12,204	9,640	31,950	20,846
China	2,867	10,994	7,864	9,655	0
Spain	7,245	5,974	5,898	5,978	635
Venezuela	13,884	6,190	5,390	5,045	1,046
Taiwan	3,479	6,497	4,500	4,643	664
Subtotal	40,169	41,859	33,293	57,271	23,190
Percent of Total	45.9%	35.3%	34.8%	64.2%	85.5%
All Buyers					
United States	12,695	12,204	9,640	31,950	20,846
Total N. America	12,695	12,204	9,640	31,950	20,846
Austria	5	0	0	2	0
Belgium	167	962	671	864	73
Finland	0	22	22	0	0
France	180	125	105	379	90
Germany	83	352	352	378	0
Greece	39	80	80	63	0
Ireland	50	42	0	22	0
Italy	986	553	473	757	50
Malta	0	0	0	2	2
Netherlands	1,028	1,421	1,403	956	0
Portugal	71	50	50	85	0
Spain	7,245	5,974	5,898	5,978	635
Sweden	43	86	65	0	0
United Kingdom	950	1,461	1,094	1,017	45
Total W. Europe	10,847	11,127	10,212	10,503	895

Canadian Split Pea Exports April, 2014
(metric tons)

Crop Year	2011-12	2012-13	2012-13	2013-14	2014
Period	Aug-Jul	Aug-Jul	Aug-Apr	Aug-Apr	Apr
Armenia	22	0	0	12	0
Bosnia and Herzegovina	0	10	10	0	0
Croatia	64	4	4	26	26
Georgia	3	50	50	103	50
Russia	167	227	103	283	0
Total E. Europe	255	290	166	424	76
Egypt	0	673	673	553	0
Ethiopia	0	0	0	1,276	0
Iraq	105	0	0	0	0
Israel	844	353	256	526	25
Kuwait	100	0	0	0	0
Oman	125	0	0	0	0
Saudi Arabia	50	50	50	121	0
Somalia	1,100	0	0	0	0
Turkey	0	50	50	105	0
United Arab Emirates	1,124	0	0	0	0
Yemen	0	0	0	75	0
Total Middle East	3,448	1,127	1,029	2,655	25
Algeria	1,166	3,796	3,796	2,816	0
Cameroon	50	100	0	1,000	650
Chad	25	0	0	0	0
Congo Democratic Republic (Zaire)	0	650	0	0	0
Cote D'ivoire	0	100	0	0	0
Djibouti	0	0	0	25	0
Gambia	25	0	0	0	0
Kenya	125	5,209	3,709	0	0
Liberia	25	0	0	0	0
Madagascar	0	0	0	75	0
Mauritania	0	450	0	0	0
Mauritius	69	205	100	25	0
Morocco	276	125	125	799	0
Saint Helena	0	26	26	0	0
Senegal	100	79	0	425	0
Sierra Leone	75	0	0	0	0
South Africa	2,619	2,639	2,564	1,848	100
Togo	700	0	0	0	0
Uganda	0	200	0	0	0
Total Africa	5,256	13,579	10,320	7,013	750

Canadian Split Pea Exports April, 2014
(metric tons)

Crop Year Period	2011-12 Aug-Jul	2012-13 Aug-Jul	2012-13 Aug-Apr	2013-14 Aug-Apr	2014 Apr
Bangladesh	0	43	0	86	0
Cambodia	0	289	0	0	0
China	2,867	10,994	7,864	9,655	0
Hong Kong	0	4	4	0	0
India	8,357	32,821	32,777	1,173	0
Indonesia	177	108	108	0	0
Japan	898	782	536	759	113
Korea South	322	131	65	0	0
Malaysia	269	1,186	773	1,838	461
Nepal	0	154	0	110	0
Pakistan	185	3,200	0	1,936	1,111
Philippines	2,322	1,140	745	890	105
Singapore	0	8	8	0	0
Sri Lanka	50	74	74	47	0
Taiwan	3,479	6,497	4,500	4,643	664
Thailand	532	68	25	863	0
Total Asia	19,458	57,499	47,480	21,999	2,452
Australia	964	262	83	87	74
Fiji	680	278	253	75	25
New Zealand	6	0	0	25	0
Total Pacific	1,650	540	336	187	99
Argentina	0	21	0	0	0
Brazil	2,290	3,469	1,455	600	251
Chile	1,695	1,337	888	565	46
Colombia	350	1,660	1,660	0	0
Ecuador	399	79	54	143	50
Guyana	1,523	715	532	591	121
Paraguay	7	3	3	0	0
Peru	5,501	2,288	1,988	4,151	105
Suriname	618	434	356	387	71
Uruguay	6	0	0	9	0
Venezuela	13,884	6,190	5,390	5,045	1,046
Total S. America	26,274	16,197	12,327	11,491	1,691

Canadian Split Pea Exports April, 2014
(metric tons)

Crop Year	2011-12	2012-13	2012-13	2013-14	2014
Period	Aug-Jul	Aug-Jul	Aug-Apr	Aug-Apr	Apr
Antigua and Barbuda	1	4	2	0	0
Aruba	1	0	0	0	0
Barbados	88	35	35	57	1
Belize	61	64	30	0	0
Costa Rica	27	3	3	0	0
Cuba	0	15	15	0	0
Dominica	2	4	3	0	0
Dominican Republic	9	10	10	1	0
Grenada	23	92	87	10	0
Jamaica	2	2	2	0	0
Mexico	3,114	1,958	1,407	1,152	99
Panama	741	560	349	462	100
Saint Lucia	2	2	1	0	0
Saint Vincent and the Grenadines	0	1	1	0	0
Trinidad	3,590	3,243	2,152	1,300	76
Total C. America	7,661	5,991	4,098	2,981	276
Total World	87,544	118,553	95,608	89,202	27,109

Source: Statistics Canada

U.S. Split Pea Exports April, 2014

(metric tons)

Crop Year	2011-12	2012-13	2012-13	2013-14	2014
Period	Sep-Aug	Sep-Aug	Sep-Apr	Sep-Apr	Apr
Top Five Buyers					
Peru	9,794	11,512	8,470	8,770	730
Sudan	598	230	230	8,768	1,784
Kenya	9,438	16,493	11,592	8,145	0
Ethiopia	19,456	8,487	8,487	6,446	0
Pakistan	11,409	5,707	4,604	2,005	0
Subtotal	50,696	42,428	33,383	34,134	2,514
Percent of Total	61.9%	57.1%	60.5%	76.4%	71.5%
All Buyers					
Canada	357	1,288	701	484	11
Total N. America	357	1,288	701	484	11
Belgium	70	0	0	106	0
France	8	0	0	283	0
Iceland	70	0	0	0	0
Italy	121	308	260	334	0
Netherlands	425	233	57	502	5
Spain	1,840	0	0	0	0
United Kingdom	2	64	64	0	0
Total W. Europe	2,535	605	381	1,225	5
Russia	1,325	1,290	903	1,118	0
Total E. Europe	1,325	1,290	903	1,118	0
Ethiopia	19,456	8,487	8,487	6,446	0
Israel	362	263	239	313	24
Somalia	1,155	195	195	0	0
Sudan	598	230	230	8,768	1,784
Yemen	501	1,093	0	371	0
Total Middle East	22,072	10,267	9,151	15,898	1,808
Algeria	0	0	0	561	0
Benin	0	300	300	0	0
Cameroon	1,640	4,102	3,471	201	0
Chad	4,343	0	0	0	0
Congo Democratic Republic (Zaire)	709	0	0	0	0
Cote D'ivoire	60	1,203	0	0	0
Djibouti	5,081	6,923	4,057	170	0
Ghana	0	60	60	0	0
Kenya	9,438	16,493	11,592	8,145	0
Liberia	520	1,171	700	901	0
Mali	2,402	419	419	134	134
Mauritania	0	399	399	0	0

U.S. Split Pea Exports April, 2014

(metric tons)

Crop Year	2011-12	2012-13	2012-13	2013-14	2014
Period	Sep-Aug	Sep-Aug	Sep-Apr	Sep-Apr	Apr
Mozambique	999	300	300	0	0
Niger	250	210	80	100	0
Senegal	0	649	649	0	0
South Africa	1,998	1,063	625	722	0
Tanzania	450	2,202	2,202	0	0
Togo	0	1,610	1,610	630	630
Zimbabwe	1,316	0	0	0	0
Total Africa	29,207	37,104	26,464	11,564	764
Bangladesh	1,723	260	0	959	0
Cambodia	444	0	0	211	0
China	338	374	374	544	0
Hong Kong	113	28	23	40	0
India	101	91	91	0	0
Japan	0	11	11	6	0
Korea South	0	204	68	0	0
Laos	0	405	0	0	0
Pakistan	11,409	5,707	4,604	2,005	0
Philippines	591	799	799	104	0
Singapore	1	0	0	0	0
Sri Lanka	1,000	475	475	0	0
Taiwan	183	0	0	0	0
Total Asia	15,903	8,354	6,444	3,869	0
Australia	102	816	795	260	23
Total Pacific	102	816	795	260	23
Brazil	0	860	813	71	0
Chile	50	0	0	48	0
Colombia	29	0	0	0	0
Peru	9,794	11,512	8,470	8,770	730
Suriname	0	0	0	63	0
Total S. America	9,873	12,372	9,283	8,952	730
Barbados	217	202	124	201	0
Bermuda	0	14	14	24	0
Guatemala	0	6	6	0	0
Mexico	309	1,925	919	1,073	173
Netherlands Antilles	8	10	5	10	2
Total C. America	534	2,158	1,069	1,308	176
Total World	81,908	74,253	55,189	44,677	3,516

Source: U.S. Department of Commerce

Australian Split Pea Exports April, 2014

(metric tons)

Crop Year	2011-12	2012-13	2012-13	2013-14	2014
Period	Nov-Oct	Nov-Oct	Nov-Apr	Nov-Apr	Apr
Top Five Buyers					
Sri Lanka	23,193	22,824	11,712	13,008	2,400
Malaysia	6,239	5,105	2,315	2,051	238
Mauritius	2,963	2,692	1,031	1,236	187
Fiji	792	668	360	1,224	0
India	375	382	382	1,076	0
Subtotal	33,563	31,671	15,801	18,594	2,825
Percent of Total	96.7%	99.0%	99.1%	98.6%	99.9%
All Buyers					
Belgium	90	0	0	0	0
United Kingdom	72	0	0	0	0
Total W. Europe	162	0	0	0	0
Israel	100	0	0	0	0
Saudi Arabia	192	96	96	92	0
United Arab Emirates	96	2	0	0	0
Yemen	48	0	0	0	0
Total Middle East	436	98	96	92	0
Mauritius	2,963	2,692	1,031	1,236	187
Total Africa	2,963	2,692	1,031	1,236	187
India	375	382	382	1,076	0
Indonesia	96	24	24	0	0
Japan	0	22	0	86	0
Malaysia	6,239	5,105	2,315	2,051	238
Singapore	24	72	24	48	0
Sri Lanka	23,193	22,824	11,712	13,008	2,400
Taiwan	0	66	0	0	0
Thailand	432	0	0	0	0
Total Asia	30,359	28,494	14,457	16,269	2,638
Fiji	792	668	360	1,224	0
New Zealand	0	24	0	34	0
Papua New Guinea	0	5	3	3	2
Total Pacific	792	697	363	1,261	2
Total World	34,713	31,981	15,948	18,858	2,827

Source: Australia Bureau of Statistics

Canadian All Whole & Split Pea Exports April, 2014

(metric tons)

Crop Year	2011-12	2012-13	2012-13	2013-14	2014
Period	Aug-Jul	Aug-Jul	Aug-Apr	Aug-Apr	Apr
Top Five Buyers					
China	651,302	750,280	515,808	851,174	13,978
India	917,965	1,005,070	852,184	640,475	13,050
United States	57,509	99,023	74,422	128,060	39,603
Bangladesh	156,357	433,987	309,970	78,781	0
United Arab Emirates	19,264	24,296	12,840	33,881	2,289
Subtotal	1,802,397	2,312,656	1,765,224	1,732,370	68,920
Percent of Total	85.9%	87.1%	87.2%	88.5%	69.6%
All Buyers					
United States	57,509	99,023	74,422	128,060	39,603
Total N. America	57,509	99,023	74,422	128,060	39,603
Austria	7	0	0	4	0
Belgium	1,194	34,720	34,392	12,153	333
Denmark	69	495	495	0	0
Finland	0	22	22	0	0
France	269	582	538	1,627	660
Germany	1,600	1,244	1,230	863	0
Greece	50	93	93	89	0
Iceland	0	22	0	72	0
Ireland	71	13,589	47	43	21
Italy	1,871	2,668	2,588	2,415	50
Malta	187	22	22	72	25
Netherlands	1,349	2,343	2,298	2,305	0
Norway	0	0	0	3,399	0
Portugal	126	126	126	572	25
Spain	13,910	53,152	53,033	7,457	660
Sweden	95	133	90	65	22
Switzerland	40	131	131	0	0
United Kingdom	1,533	5,145	4,166	1,804	45
Total W. Europe	22,369	114,488	99,270	32,941	1,841

Canadian All Whole & Split Pea Exports April, 2014

(metric tons)

Crop Year	2011-12	2012-13	2012-13	2013-14	2014
Period	Aug-Jul	Aug-Jul	Aug-Apr	Aug-Apr	Apr
Armenia	70	0	0	37	0
Bosnia and Herzegovina	0	10	10	0	0
Bulgaria	0	0	0	75	0
Croatia	82	4	4	26	26
Czech Republic	25	25	25	47	22
Estonia	0	100	100	0	0
Georgia	94	100	100	145	50
Poland	0	0	0	274	0
Romania	0	0	0	184	0
Russia	888	2,208	2,041	1,586	0
Total E. Europe	1,160	2,445	2,278	2,375	98
Bahrain	0	0	0	75	0
Egypt	1,631	2,614	2,614	7,025	1,607
Ethiopia	0	0	0	1,276	0
Iraq	105	0	0	0	0
Israel	1,179	757	660	2,013	75
Jordan	244	138	138	347	0
Kuwait	299	0	0	76	25
Lebanon	0	120	118	98	0
Libya	0	0	0	409	23
Oman	370	249	249	0	0
Saudi Arabia	3,674	2,664	2,664	2,333	263
Somalia	1,100	0	0	0	0
Turkey	25	239	239	1,465	105
United Arab Emirates	19,264	24,296	12,840	33,881	2,289
Yemen	6,053	5,216	4,460	7,886	352
Total Middle East	33,945	36,293	23,983	56,883	4,737
Algeria	2,427	5,359	5,359	5,880	103
Burkina Faso	1	1	1	1	0
Cameroon	50	100	0	1,000	650
Chad	25	0	0	0	0
Congo Democratic Republic (Zaire)	0	650	0	0	0
Cote D'ivoire	0	275	175	0	0
Djibouti	200	0	0	25	0
Gambia	25	0	0	125	0
Kenya	125	5,209	3,709	0	0
Liberia	25	389	173	497	0
Madagascar	0	351	351	75	0

Canadian All Whole & Split Pea Exports April, 2014

(metric tons)

Crop Year	2011-12	2012-13	2012-13	2013-14	2014
Period	Aug-Jul	Aug-Jul	Aug-Apr	Aug-Apr	Apr
Mauritania	375	450	0	0	0
Mauritius	271	290	155	376	0
Morocco	640	365	185	2,542	229
Saint Helena	0	26	26	0	0
Senegal	338	3,043	1,572	3,064	0
Sierra Leone	75	0	0	0	0
South Africa	5,283	4,593	4,274	3,776	246
Togo	700	0	0	0	0
Tunisia	248	95	95	229	0
Uganda	0	200	0	0	0
Total Africa	10,808	21,396	16,074	17,589	1,227
Bangladesh	156,357	433,987	309,970	78,781	0
Cambodia	664	606	316	317	45
China	651,302	750,280	515,808	851,174	13,978
Hong Kong	0	6	6	0	0
India	917,965	1,005,070	852,184	640,475	13,050
Indonesia	31,132	16,324	14,174	11,686	3,380
Japan	6,383	5,105	3,689	8,727	2,697
Korea South	498	131	65	0	0
Macau	0	0	0	90	0
Malaysia	562	1,235	821	2,203	508
Myanmar	0	0	0	132	0
Nepal	3,601	7,306	6,586	2,851	124
Pakistan	1,940	6,206	2,657	10,272	4,930
Philippines	19,755	12,280	8,019	16,300	2,738
Singapore	193	9	9	800	0
Sri Lanka	987	963	755	932	0
Taiwan	10,899	11,759	8,992	9,227	1,095
Thailand	2,457	1,669	1,338	2,598	151
Vietnam	175	21	21	452	0
Total Asia	1,804,871	2,252,958	1,725,410	1,637,015	42,696
Australia	1,269	262	83	1,038	665
Christmas Island	0	188	0	0	0
Fiji	1,319	405	381	402	50
New Zealand	29	20	0	144	0
U.S. Minor Outlying Islands	0	0	0	142	135
Total Pacific	2,617	875	463	1,726	850

Canadian All Whole & Split Pea Exports April, 2014

(metric tons)

Crop Year	2011-12	2012-13	2012-13	2013-14	2014
Period	Aug-Jul	Aug-Jul	Aug-Apr	Aug-Apr	Apr
Argentina	20	277	256	250	0
Brazil	4,426	12,090	8,506	4,397	800
Chile	4,890	3,759	3,082	4,578	531
Colombia	30,741	21,694	18,378	15,269	2,568
Ecuador	3,575	2,355	1,816	2,572	387
Guyana	2,812	2,580	1,744	1,442	253
Paraguay	7	3	3	0	0
Peru	13,808	7,934	6,815	8,271	369
Suriname	894	924	846	615	228
Uruguay	6	0	0	25	0
Venezuela	23,411	14,869	9,812	18,418	1,718
Total S. America	84,589	66,484	51,258	55,837	6,854
Antigua and Barbuda	9	11	5	11	3
Aruba	2	0	0	1	0
Barbados	119	36	36	77	1
Belize	112	69	30	74	8
Costa Rica	529	316	250	373	96
Cuba	66,000	48,015	22,015	18,354	354
Dominica	18	11	6	10	0
Dominican Republic	114	61	61	196	0
Grenada	128	128	93	66	1
Haiti	0	550	550	0	0
Jamaica	4	2	2	0	0
Mexico	7,545	5,651	4,959	2,426	240
Panama	1,849	995	758	592	100
Saint Lucia	5	2	2	1	0
Saint Vincent and the Grenadines	5	2	1	7	0
Trinidad	4,622	4,703	3,055	2,715	331
Total C. America	81,061	60,553	31,825	24,903	1,135
Total World	2,098,929	2,654,515	2,024,983	1,957,330	99,041

Source: Statistics Canada

Australian Whole Pea Exports April, 2014

(metric tons)

Crop Year	2011-12	2012-13	2012-13	2013-14	2014
Period	Nov-Oct	Nov-Oct	Nov-Apr	Nov-Apr	Apr
Top Five Buyers					
India	119,868	74,937	45,382	44,872	8,861
Bangladesh	0	13,647	13,017	8,102	6,600
Malaysia	22,052	16,448	9,139	3,322	563
Philippines	4,057	3,832	2,196	3,290	465
Belgium	4,447	5,381	3,182	2,474	384
Subtotal	150,424	114,243	72,916	62,060	16,873
Percent of Total	88.5%	84.4%	88.0%	92.0%	96.3%
All Buyers					
Belgium	4,447	5,381	3,182	2,474	384
Germany	0	0	0	27	0
Ireland	0	48	48	75	25
Italy	25	24	24	28	0
Netherlands	99	304	208	267	107
Portugal	124	172	124	72	44
United Kingdom	47	958	557	292	25
Total W. Europe	4,742	6,887	4,144	3,233	585
Egypt	0	0	0	102	0
Israel	24	23	23	0	0
Jordan	8	22	22	0	0
Kuwait	48	51	51	71	0
Saudi Arabia	250	0	0	0	0
United Arab Emirates	0	0	0	117	0
Yemen	1,441	1,929	1,057	1,112	142
Total Middle East	1,771	2,025	1,153	1,402	142
Mauritius	280	264	24	47	0
South Africa	23	0	0	48	24
Total Africa	303	264	24	95	24

Australian Whole Pea Exports April, 2014

(metric tons)

Crop Year	2011-12	2012-13	2012-13	2013-14	2014
Period	Nov-Oct	Nov-Oct	Nov-Apr	Nov-Apr	Apr
Bangladesh	0	13,647	13,017	8,102	6,600
China	2,135	49	0	0	0
Hong Kong	179	253	138	184	0
India	119,868	74,937	45,382	44,872	8,861
Indonesia	42	0	0	0	0
Japan	1,107	1,198	577	664	153
Malaysia	22,052	16,448	9,139	3,322	563
Pakistan	2,673	0	0	0	0
Philippines	4,057	3,832	2,196	3,290	465
Sri Lanka	3,767	5,220	2,848	428	0
Taiwan	2,324	2,660	1,319	1,889	120
Thailand	0	12	12	9	9
Vietnam	160	0	0	0	0
Total Asia	158,364	118,255	74,628	62,760	16,771
Fiji	4,751	7,811	2,870	0	0
New Caledonia	0	3	1	0	0
Total Pacific	4,751	7,814	2,871	0	0
Argentina	0	22	0	0	0
Chile	17	17	0	0	0
Total S. America	17	39	0	0	0
Total World	169,947	135,284	82,820	67,490	17,522

Source: Australia Bureau of Statistics

Yellow Peas

Canadian Yellow Pea Supply and Demand Estimates
(metric tons, acres)

Year	2010	2011	2012	2013	2014
Area (acres)	2,990,000	2,052,000	3,300,000	2,835,000	3,435,000
Yield (lbs)	1,849	2,312	1,943	2,551	2,116
Production	2,508,000	2,152,200	2,909,000	3,279,900	3,296,500
Carry In	809,000	427,000	263,000	162,000	359,200
Imports	30,700	9,300	13,200	17,700	17,700
Stocks	3,347,700	2,588,500	3,185,200	3,459,600	3,673,400
Disappearance					
Export	2,573,635	1,766,835	2,355,785	2,164,000	2,255,000
Seed	144,000	232,000	199,000	242,000	184,000
Feed & Waste	203,066	326,665	468,416	694,400	527,600
Total Usage	2,920,701	2,325,500	3,023,201	3,100,400	2,966,600
Ending Stock	427,000	263,000	162,000	359,200	706,800
Stocks/Use	14.6%	11.3%	5.4%	11.6%	23.8%

Forecasts by STAT Market Research based on data from Statistics Canada

Canadian Yellow Pea Exports April, 2014

(metric tons)

Crop Year	2011-12	2012-13	2012-13	2013-14	2014
Period	Aug-Jul	Aug-Jul	Aug-Apr	Aug-Apr	Apr
Top Five Buyers					
China	561,794	675,015	443,943	768,043	11,912
India	858,945	941,203	792,393	577,256	8,504
Bangladesh	156,256	433,844	309,970	78,695	0
United States	11,899	38,460	31,348	33,878	8,028
United Arab Emirates	11,077	20,110	9,560	24,694	1,249
Subtotal	1,599,971	2,108,632	1,587,214	1,482,566	29,693
Percent of Total	92.5%	91.8%	92.1%	95.7%	69.3%
All Buyers					
United States	11,899	38,460	31,348	33,878	8,028
Total N. America	11,899	38,460	31,348	33,878	8,028
Belgium	1,004	31,437	31,437	43	0
Germany	452	0	0	0	0
Greece	5	0	0	0	0
Ireland	0	13,500	0	0	0
Italy	43	375	375	74	0
Malta	2	1	1	2	0
Netherlands	70	521	494	187	0
Norway	0	0	0	3,374	0
Spain	0	36,524	36,524	25	0
Sweden	0	25	25	0	0
Switzerland	40	0	0	0	0
United Kingdom	532	704	603	134	0
Total W. Europe	2,148	83,086	69,459	3,838	0
Armenia	24	0	0	0	0
Estonia	0	100	100	0	0
Georgia	50	46	46	42	0
Romania	0	0	0	26	0
Russia	50	143	100	0	0
Total E. Europe	124	289	245	69	0
Bahrain	0	0	0	25	0
Egypt	0	0	0	631	493
Israel	24	89	89	203	0
Kuwait	50	0	0	50	25
Lebanon	0	43	43	0	0
Oman	245	249	249	0	0
Turkey	0	0	0	1,025	105
United Arab Emirates	11,077	20,110	9,560	24,694	1,249
Total Middle East	11,396	20,491	9,941	26,627	1,872

Canadian Yellow Pea Exports April, 2014

(metric tons)

Crop Year	2011-12	2012-13	2012-13	2013-14	2014
Period	Aug-Jul	Aug-Jul	Aug-Apr	Aug-Apr	Apr
Cote D'ivoire	0	175	175	0	0
Djibouti	200	0	0	0	0
Liberia	0	389	173	497	0
Madagascar	0	351	351	0	0
Mauritania	225	0	0	0	0
Mauritius	77	75	45	213	0
Morocco	0	0	0	50	0
Senegal	0	1,257	150	0	0
South Africa	442	566	541	382	46
Total Africa	944	2,813	1,435	1,142	46
Bangladesh	156,256	433,844	309,970	78,695	0
China	561,794	675,015	443,943	768,043	11,912
India	858,945	941,203	792,393	577,256	8,504
Indonesia	28,033	15,865	13,715	11,524	3,380
Japan	1,653	1,828	1,282	5,566	2,236
Korea South	65	0	0	0	0
Myanmar	0	0	0	132	0
Nepal	0	4,853	4,287	1,470	124
Pakistan	1,245	2,500	2,150	7,437	3,689
Philippines	2,553	3,228	1,828	2,990	514
Singapore	0	2	2	0	0
Sri Lanka	0	278	278	275	0
Taiwan	5,685	4,114	3,343	1,996	47
Thailand	194	143	131	409	43
Total Asia	1,616,423	2,082,873	1,573,322	1,455,793	30,451
Australia	21	0	0	822	548
Christmas Island	0	188	0	0	0
New Zealand	0	20	0	20	0
U.S. Minor Outlying Islands	0	0	0	140	135
Total Pacific	21	208	0	981	683
Chile	25	76	76	705	0
Colombia	6,529	7,286	5,739	2,975	652
Ecuador	1,421	1,230	814	975	144
Guyana	1,057	1,057	823	275	79
Peru	4,354	3,870	3,130	2,023	264
Suriname	276	310	310	42	0
Venezuela	1,844	1,677	736	1,002	0
Total S. America	15,507	15,507	11,628	7,997	1,139

Canadian Yellow Pea Exports April, 2014

(metric tons)

Crop Year	2011-12	2012-13	2012-13	2013-14	2014
Period	Aug-Jul	Aug-Jul	Aug-Apr	Aug-Apr	Apr
Antigua and Barbuda	1	0	0	0	0
Barbados	25	0	0	0	0
Belize	47	0	0	0	0
Costa Rica	0	4	4	0	0
Cuba	66,000	48,000	22,000	18,354	354
Dominica	2	0	0	0	0
Grenada	68	0	0	0	0
Mexico	3,899	3,493	3,353	609	142
Panama	868	378	351	79	0
Saint Lucia	1	0	0	0	0
Saint Vincent and the Grenadines	1	0	0	0	0
Trinidad	948	483	351	368	158
Total C. America	71,860	52,357	26,059	19,410	653
Total World	1,730,321	2,296,084	1,723,437	1,549,735	42,871

Source: Statistics Canada

U.S. Yellow Pea Exports April, 2014

(metric tons)

Crop Year	2011-12	2012-13	2012-13	2013-14	2014
Period	Sep-Aug	Sep-Aug	Sep-Apr	Sep-Apr	Apr
Top Five Buyers					
India	46,297	4,902	4,527	68,639	2,260
China	1,236	4,618	3,551	16,551	1,617
Ethiopia	1,921	0	0	5,019	0
Pakistan	2,744	6,762	2,429	2,593	130
Tanzania	0	2,140	2,140	1,751	839
Subtotal	52,198	18,422	12,647	94,553	4,845
Percent of Total	78.5%	35.0%	34.1%	92.7%	83.8%
All Buyers					
Canada	1,888	670	670	585	209
Total N. America	1,888	670	670	585	209
Belgium	3,030	5,454	3,628	0	0
Denmark	0	0	0	422	0
Germany	49	45	45	0	0
Iceland	0	76	76	0	0
United Kingdom	0	0	0	42	0
Total W. Europe	3,079	5,576	3,749	465	0
Kyrgyzstan	0	173	173	80	0
Total E. Europe	0	173	173	80	0
Ethiopia	1,921	0	0	5,019	0
Total Middle East	1,921	0	0	5,019	0
Algeria	0	887	887	0	0
Burkina Faso	224	0	0	0	0
Burundi	110	0	0	0	0
Cameroon	0	1,728	0	0	0
Central African Republic	134	0	0	0	0
Djibouti	0	5,869	1,308	0	0
Kenya	138	2,339	2,339	0	0
Mali	321	0	0	0	0
Mozambique	0	4,039	4,039	0	0
Niger	268	0	0	0	0
South Africa	0	4,891	4,891	1,391	0
Tanzania	0	2,140	2,140	1,751	839
Uganda	277	187	100	0	0
Zimbabwe	830	0	0	0	0
Total Africa	2,301	22,079	15,704	3,142	839

U.S. Yellow Pea Exports April, 2014
(metric tons)

Crop Year Period	2011-12 Sep-Aug	2012-13 Sep-Aug	2012-13 Sep-Apr	2013-14 Sep-Apr	2014 Apr
Afghanistan	843	830	830	0	0
Bangladesh	389	0	0	0	0
China	1,236	4,618	3,551	16,551	1,617
Hong Kong	0	19	19	0	0
India	46,297	4,902	4,527	68,639	2,260
Indonesia	2,123	2,385	2,113	1,028	0
Korea South	87	1,111	954	1,688	0
Malaysia	2	48	0	0	0
Pakistan	2,744	6,762	2,429	2,593	130
Philippines	0	407	99	116	0
Taiwan	2,865	1,539	1,477	1,100	366
Thailand	32	25	25	30	0
Total Asia	56,618	22,645	16,023	91,746	4,373
South Georgia and the South Sandwich Islands	0	68	0	0	0
Total Pacific	0	68	0	0	0
Colombia	250	414	344	420	0
Peru	0	0	0	365	365
Suriname	4	16	11	8	0
Total S. America	255	431	355	793	365
Dominican Republic	13	63	46	0	0
Haiti	423	787	192	0	0
Jamaica	23	9	9	8	0
Leeward Windward Is.	0	21	21	9	0
Mexico	0	0	0	12	0
Panama	0	0	0	50	0
Trinidad	0	168	168	113	0
Total C. America	459	1,048	436	192	0
Total World	66,520	52,689	37,109	102,019	5,785

Source: U.S. Department of Commerce

Other Peas

U.S. Pea (nes) Exports April, 2014
(metric tons)

Crop Year	2011-12	2012-13	2012-13	2013-14	2014
Period	Sep-Aug	Sep-Aug	Sep-Apr	Sep-Apr	Apr
Top Five Buyers					
Djibouti	3,741	2,381	529	10,491	0
India	10,991	9,818	7,844	9,745	1,543
Ethiopia	7,192	0	0	6,575	168
South Africa	3,423	3,379	2,285	4,988	0
Philippines	3,492	9,021	7,207	4,562	525
Subtotal	28,839	24,600	17,864	36,361	2,236
Percent of Total	52.4%	55.9%	55.4%	66.1%	45.3%
All Buyers					
Canada	1,639	2,744	1,776	1,300	215
Total N. America	1,639	2,744	1,776	1,300	215
Belgium	0	473	382	426	45
Denmark	229	0	0	210	0
France	0	0	0	25	0
Germany	0	10	10	0	0
Iceland	21	41	41	0	0
Italy	0	0	0	71	0
Netherlands	0	20	20	87	0
Spain	2,864	1,049	1,049	0	0
United Kingdom	0	462	462	0	0
Total W. Europe	3,113	2,055	1,964	820	45
Estonia	0	0	0	68	68
Total E. Europe	0	0	0	68	68
Egypt	2	0	0	253	0
Ethiopia	7,192	0	0	6,575	168
Lebanon	0	151	151	0	0
Somalia	755	0	0	1,155	993
Sudan	0	1,138	1,138	0	0
Turkey	229	0	0	0	0
United Arab Emirates	281	327	22	92	0
Total Middle East	8,459	1,615	1,310	8,074	1,161

U.S. Pea (nes) Exports April, 2014

(metric tons)

Crop Year	2011-12	2012-13	2012-13	2013-14	2014
Period	Sep-Aug	Sep-Aug	Sep-Apr	Sep-Apr	Apr
Algeria	0	0	0	211	0
Burkina Faso	1,121	350	0	550	0
Burundi	420	0	0	0	0
Chad	997	0	0	964	0
Congo Democratic Republic (Zaire)	1,427	0	0	0	0
Djibouti	3,741	2,381	529	10,491	0
Kenya	5,795	4,442	3,722	3,220	0
Malawi	0	0	0	575	0
Mauritania	0	206	206	0	0
Rwanda	90	0	0	0	0
South Africa	3,423	3,379	2,285	4,988	0
Uganda	720	0	0	0	0
Total Africa	17,732	10,759	6,743	20,999	0
China	1,973	2,545	1,705	2,654	0
Hong Kong	24	87	2	54	0
India	10,991	9,818	7,844	9,745	1,543
Japan	57	282	43	23	0
Korea South	409	301	139	116	0
Malaysia	70	302	232	46	0
Nepal	0	0	0	158	0
Pakistan	0	299	299	187	187
Philippines	3,492	9,021	7,207	4,562	525
Sri Lanka	2,272	300	290	1,112	129
Taiwan	0	300	300	1,362	0
Total Asia	19,288	23,255	18,061	20,020	2,384
Australia	62	0	0	41	0
New Zealand	0	68	68	0	0
Total Pacific	62	68	68	41	0
Argentina	0	9	9	0	0
Brazil	0	24	24	0	0
Chile	0	0	0	747	333
Colombia	23	475	475	474	401
Ecuador	0	99	99	42	0
Peru	985	358	217	587	164
Suriname	0	5	5	0	0
Total S. America	1,008	969	827	1,850	898

U.S. Pea (nes) Exports April, 2014

(metric tons)

Crop Year	2011-12	2012-13	2012-13	2013-14	2014
Period	Sep-Aug	Sep-Aug	Sep-Apr	Sep-Apr	Apr
Bahamas	0	15	15	0	0
Barbados	73	34	32	14	0
Dominican Republic	0	0	0	9	0
Haiti	126	20	0	20	20
Honduras	24	0	0	0	0
Jamaica	5	1	1	0	0
Leeward Windward Is.	1,012	222	214	12	0
Mexico	2,465	2,248	1,253	1,757	149
Netherlands Antilles	0	0	0	1	0
Panama	0	0	0	24	0
Trinidad	0	6	0	8	0
Turks and Caicos Islands	0	3	3	0	0
Total C. America	3,705	2,549	1,518	1,844	169
Total World	55,005	44,013	32,266	55,016	4,939

Source: U.S. Department of Commerce

U.S. Austrian Winter (Black) Pea Exports April, 2014

(metric tons)

Crop Year	2011-12	2012-13	2012-13	2013-14	2014
Period	Sep-Aug	Sep-Aug	Sep-Apr	Sep-Apr	Apr
Bahamas	0	0	0	2	0
India	0	3,738	2,216	180	0
Japan	273	104	104	246	0
Philippines	0	24	0	0	0
Taiwan	520	650	626	208	0
Total World	793	4,516	2,947	636	0

Source: U.S. Department of Commerce

U.S. Pigeon Pea Exports April, 2014

(metric tons)

Crop Year	2011-12	2012-13	2012-13	2013-14	2014
Period	Sep-Aug	Sep-Aug	Sep-Apr	Sep-Apr	Apr
Barbados	0	0	0	5	0
Canada	47	24	5	0	0
Leeward Windward Is.	0	1	1	2	0
Netherlands Antilles	6	3	3	5	5
Total World	53	28	10	12	5

Source: U.S. Department of Commerce

Canadian Pigeon Pea Exports April, 2014
(metric tons)

Crop Year	2011-12	2012-13	2012-13	2013-14	2014
Period	Aug-Jul	Aug-Jul	Aug-Apr	Aug-Apr	Apr
Antigua and Barbuda	1	3	2	0	0
Barbados	0	3	3	0	0
Dominica	1	6	6	0	0
Grenada	0	12	12	0	0
India	0	17	17	0	0
Jamaica	3	3	3	0	0
Trinidad	2	8	8	0	0
United Arab Emirates	0	0	0	22	22
United States	0	11	11	6	1
Total World	6	63	62	27	23

Source: Statistics Canada

Chickpeas

World Chickpea Production Summary

(hectares, metric tons, kilograms)

Area (acres)	2010	2011	2012	2013	2014
Australia	1,350,000	1,127,000	1,418,000	1,253,000	1,268,000
Canada	210,000	118,000	200,000	191,000	106,000
United States	146,000	136,000	208,000	216,000	218,000
Turkey	1,103,000	1,103,000	1,029,000	890,000	845,000
Spain	74,000	62,000	64,000	67,000	64,000
Mexico	220,000	119,000	321,000	219,000	197,000
Morocco	193,000	219,000	125,000	184,000	198,000
Syria	169,000	184,000	185,000	91,000	49,000
Pakistan	2,636,000	2,604,000	2,607,000	2,663,000	2,615,000
India	20,287,000	22,758,000	22,701,000	23,512,000	25,553,000
Other	3,484,000	3,762,000	3,537,000	3,532,000	3,619,000
Total	29,872,000	32,192,000	32,395,000	32,818,000	34,732,000
Production (MT)	2010	2011	2012	2013	2014
Australia	462,000	673,000	813,000	629,000	663,000
Canada	131,000	86,000	162,000	180,000	82,000
United States	88,000	100,000	151,000	157,000	154,000
Turkey	531,000	487,000	535,000	325,000	390,000
Spain	25,000	22,000	23,000	24,000	22,000
Mexico	132,000	72,000	200,000	181,000	160,000
Morocco	57,000	46,000	33,000	56,000	53,000
Syria	43,000	50,000	52,000	8,000	6,000
Pakistan	561,500	496,000	291,000	900,000	594,200
India	7,480,000	8,220,000	7,700,000	8,830,000	9,790,000
Other	1,400,000	1,599,000	1,420,000	1,398,000	1,481,000
Total	10,910,500	11,851,000	11,380,000	12,688,000	13,395,200
Yields (pounds per acre)	2010	2011	2012	2013	2014
Australia	754	1,317	1,264	1,107	1,153
Canada	1,375	1,607	1,786	2,078	1,705
United States	1,329	1,621	1,600	1,602	1,557
Turkey	1,061	973	1,146	805	1,018
Spain	745	782	792	790	758
Mexico	1,323	1,334	1,374	1,822	1,791
Morocco	651	463	582	671	590
Syria	561	599	620	194	270
Pakistan	470	420	246	745	501
India	813	796	748	828	845
Other	402	425	401	396	409
Average	805	812	774	852	850

Projections by STAT Market Research based on data from Statistics Canada, ABARE, USDA

World Chickpea Supply and Demand Situation

(hectares, metric tons, kilograms)

	2010	2011	2012	2013	2014
Area (hectares)	29,872,000	32,192,000	32,395,000	32,818,000	34,732,000
Yield (kg/ha)	365	368	351	387	386
Production	10,910,500	11,851,000	11,380,000	12,688,000	13,395,200
Carry-in	214,000	202,000	290,000	371,000	410,000
Supply	11,124,500	12,053,000	11,670,000	13,059,000	13,805,200
Trade	1,190,335	1,295,914	1,888,820	960,000	582,000
Inferred Use	10,922,500	11,763,000	11,299,000	12,649,000	13,498,200
Ending Stock	202,000	290,000	371,000	410,000	307,000
Stock-Use Ratio	1.8%	2.5%	3.3%	3.2%	2.3%
Per Capita Use (kg)	1.594	1.698	1.613	1.787	1.907

Estimates by STAT Publishing based data from the FAO, USDA, Statistics Canada, ABARES, and other entities.

World Desi Chickpea Supply and Demand Situation

(hectares, metric tons, kilograms)

	2010	2011	2012	2013	2014
Area (hectares)	10,117,000	11,040,000	11,127,000	11,410,000	12,218,000
Yield (kg/ha)	879	893	830	947	941
Production	8,891,000	9,855,000	9,238,000	10,804,000	11,493,000
Carry-in	109,000	52,000	87,000	6,000	59,000
Supply	9,000,000	9,907,000	9,325,000	10,810,000	11,552,000
Trade	737,335	914,914	1,420,820	468,000	120,000
Inferred Use	8,948,000	9,820,000	9,319,000	10,751,000	11,490,000
Ending Stock	52,000	87,000	6,000	59,000	62,000
Stock-Use Ratio	0.6%	0.9%	0.1%	0.5%	0.5%
Per Capita Use (kg)	1.306	1.417	1.331	1.519	1.623

Estimates by STAT Publishing based data from the FAO, USDA, Statistics Canada, ABARES, and other entities.

World Kabuli Chickpea Supply and Demand Situation

(hectares, metric tons, kilograms)

	2010	2011	2012	2013	2014
Area (hectares)	1,972,000	1,988,000	1,983,000	1,872,000	1,837,000
Yield (kg/ha)	1,024	1,004	1,080	1,006	1,035
Production	2,020,000	1,996,000	2,142,000	1,884,000	1,902,000
Carry-in	105,000	150,000	203,000	365,000	351,000
Supply	2,125,000	2,146,000	2,345,000	2,249,000	2,253,000
Trade	453,000	381,000	468,000	492,000	462,000
Inferred Use	1,975,000	1,943,000	1,980,000	1,898,000	2,008,000
Ending Stock	150,000	203,000	365,000	351,000	245,000
Stock-Use Ratio	7.6%	10.4%	18.4%	18.5%	12.2%
Per Capita Use (kg)	0.288	0.280	0.283	0.268	0.284

Estimates by STAT Publishing based data from the FAO, USDA, Statistics Canada, ABARES, and other entities.

Australian Chickpea Supply and Demand Estimates

(metric tons, acres)

Year	2010	2011	2012	2013	2014
Area	1,350,402	1,126,776	1,418,354	1,252,797	1,267,623
Yield (lbs)	754	1,317	1,264	1,107	1,153
Production	461,710	673,000	813,300	629,000	662,700
Carry In	106,000	55,000	91,000	5,000	49,000
Stocks	567,710	728,000	904,300	634,000	711,700
Disappearance					
Nov-Apr Exports	224,525	333,329	666,673	349,242	N/A
% of Annual	47.6 %	57.1 %	78.1 %	65.2 %	N/A
Export	471,361	584,065	853,121	536,000	599,000
Seed	36,800	46,300	40,900	42,000	45,700
Feed & Other	4,549	6,635	5,279	7,000	7,000
Total Usage	512,710	637,000	899,300	585,000	651,700
Ending Stock	55,000	91,000	5,000	49,000	60,000
Stocks/Use	10.7 %	14.3 %	0.6 %	8.4 %	9.2 %

Forecasts by STAT Market Research based on data from ABARE, ABS and Pulse Australia

U.S. Chickpea Supply and Demand Estimates

(metric tons, acres)

Year	2010	2011	2012	2013	2014
Acreage	146,000	135,800	207,900	215,700	217,800
Yield (lbs)	1,328	1,622	1,603	1,608	1,558
Production	87,952	99,882	151,139	157,353	153,905
Carryin	8,000	1,000	500	52,000	91,000
Imports	19,411	18,614	36,171	24,055	14,925
Stocks	115,363	119,496	187,809	233,407	259,829
Disappearance					
Total Exports	49,925	73,606	62,676	45,100	71,100
Domestic	56,738	33,602	59,813	77,620	67,257
Seed, Feed, Waste	7,700	11,788	13,321	19,688	21,472
Total Usage	114,363	118,996	135,810	142,408	159,829
Ending Stocks	1,000	500	52,000	91,000	100,000
Stocks/Use Ratio	0.9 %	0.4 %	38.3 %	63.9 %	62.6 %

Forecasts by STAT Publishing based on data from the USDA and U.S. Department of Commerce

Canadian Chickpea Supply and Demand Estimates

(metric tons, acres)

Year	2010	2011	2012	2013	2014
Area (acres)	210,000	117,500	200,000	190,500	106,000
Yield (lbs)	1,378	1,606	1,788	2,088	1,705
Production	131,300	85,600	162,200	180,400	82,000
Imports	8,900	6,000	7,000	7,000	7,000
Carry In	20,000	22,000	11,000	54,000	95,000
Stocks	160,200	113,600	180,200	241,400	184,000
Disappearance					
Aug-Apr Exports	74,058	31,247	56,309	26,896	N/A
Percent of Forecast	84.9 %	81.9 %	78.6 %	66.1 %	N/A
Exports	87,221	38,154	71,633	40,700	67,100
Seed	8,300	14,840	15,081	8,340	10,040
Feed & Waste	10,500	24,246	25,859	67,759	32,400
Other Domestic	32,179	25,360	13,628	29,601	29,460
Total Usage	138,200	102,600	126,201	146,400	139,000
Ending Stock	22,000	11,000	54,000	95,000	45,000
Stock/Use	15.9 %	10.7 %	42.8 %	64.9 %	32.4 %

Forecasts by STAT Market Research based on data from Statistics Canada

Australian Chickpea Exports April, 2014

(metric tons)

Crop Year	2011-12	2012-13	2012-13	2013-14	2014
Period	Nov-Oct	Nov-Oct	Nov-Apr	Nov-Apr	Apr
Top Five Buyers					
India	173,043	484,241	432,706	139,497	17,579
Bangladesh	116,300	213,394	138,794	109,217	38,538
Pakistan	189,272	42,871	29,898	33,503	3,016
United Arab Emirates	47,312	58,540	34,113	27,785	9,953
Nepal	7,649	13,456	7,131	8,733	1,564
Subtotal	533,575	812,501	642,643	318,735	70,651
Percent of Total	92.0%	95.2%	96.4%	91.3%	91.8%
All Buyers					
Canada	3,895	5,019	2,163	2,619	816
United States	2,250	3,045	1,696	2,298	409
Total N. America	6,145	8,064	3,859	4,917	1,225
Belgium	96	0	0	0	0
France	718	27	12	24	0
Germany	139	118	118	73	0
Greece	25	46	0	0	0
Italy	366	787	365	237	48
Netherlands	95	0	0	0	0
Portugal	24	155	23	2,907	48
Spain	650	97	49	284	24
Sweden	23	0	0	0	0
United Kingdom	11,712	8,480	4,475	5,397	1,337
Total W. Europe	13,849	9,709	5,041	8,922	1,457
Bahrain	12	0	0	0	0
Egypt	6,605	2,861	2,474	4,197	904
Israel	977	259	67	235	0
Jordan	2,919	1,344	420	908	243
Kuwait	460	45	23	0	0
Lebanon	493	571	571	234	0
Qatar	22	16	16	0	0
Saudi Arabia	4,840	4,837	4,013	3,830	589
Turkey	2,216	932	99	46	0
United Arab Emirates	47,312	58,540	34,113	27,785	9,953
Yemen	328	355	190	330	93
Total Middle East	66,183	69,760	41,985	37,564	11,782

Australian Chickpea Exports April, 2014

(metric tons)

Crop Year	2011-12	2012-13	2012-13	2013-14	2014
Period	Nov-Oct	Nov-Oct	Nov-Apr	Nov-Apr	Apr
Algeria	275	120	120	0	0
Kenya	45	0	0	0	0
Mauritius	1,544	1,887	1,131	896	147
South Africa	760	1,154	783	972	550
Tunisia	116	0	0	0	0
Total Africa	2,740	3,161	2,034	1,868	696
Bangladesh	116,300	213,394	138,794	109,217	38,538
Hong Kong	0	23	0	0	0
India	173,043	484,241	432,706	139,497	17,579
Indonesia	0	92	0	0	0
Japan	32	47	24	24	0
Korea South	37	19	0	0	0
Malaysia	811	2,532	1,833	693	192
Nepal	7,649	13,456	7,131	8,733	1,564
Pakistan	189,272	42,871	29,898	33,503	3,016
Philippines	0	0	0	50	0
Singapore	425	457	167	314	48
Sri Lanka	3,012	4,759	3,051	3,653	807
Taiwan	0	22	22	0	0
Thailand	243	213	70	21	0
Vietnam	0	0	0	48	0
Total Asia	490,822	762,124	613,697	295,753	61,745
Fiji	140	150	33	94	24
New Zealand	24	146	24	118	0
Papua New Guinea	4	8	0	6	0
Total Pacific	168	303	57	218	24
Guyana	121	0	0	0	0
Total S. America	121	0	0	0	0
Panama	110	0	0	0	0
Total C. America	110	0	0	0	0
Total World	580,138	853,121	666,673	349,242	76,930

Source: Australia Bureau of Statistics

Canadian Chickpea Exports April, 2014

(metric tons)

Crop Year	2011-12	2012-13	2012-13	2013-14	2014
Period	Aug-Jul	Aug-Jul	Aug-Apr	Aug-Apr	Apr
Top Five Buyers					
United States	9,674	13,766	9,332	12,053	1,577
United Kingdom	2,171	3,170	2,168	2,139	456
Jordan	3,154	2,797	2,048	1,729	414
India	3,575	1,174	394	1,308	64
Israel	1,200	3,218	2,993	1,154	43
Subtotal	19,774	24,125	16,935	18,382	2,555
Percent of Total	51.8%	33.7%	30.1%	68.3%	52.0%
All Buyers					
United States	9,674	13,766	9,332	12,053	1,577
Total N. America	9,674	13,766	9,332	12,053	1,577
Austria	5	0	0	0	0
Belgium	210	317	272	765	145
France	0	43	0	48	0
Germany	60	175	175	65	20
Greece	25	241	218	0	0
Italy	1,512	3,802	3,456	1,050	275
Netherlands	230	629	604	276	150
Portugal	299	0	0	0	0
Spain	446	3,267	2,825	962	24
Sweden	0	244	68	40	0
Switzerland	48	25	0	45	0
United Kingdom	2,171	3,170	2,168	2,139	456
Total W. Europe	5,005	11,913	9,786	5,391	1,069
Armenia	43	22	22	0	0
Bosnia and Herzegovina	0	25	25	0	0
Bulgaria	0	284	35	0	0
Croatia	0	70	70	25	0
Czech Republic	0	249	249	60	0
Hungary	0	100	0	0	0
Kazakhstan	0	53	53	0	0
Lithuania	0	21	21	0	0
Poland	41	45	20	174	69
Russia	0	75	75	50	0
Total E. Europe	84	944	570	308	69

Canadian Chickpea Exports April, 2014
(metric tons)

Crop Year	2011-12	2012-13	2012-13	2013-14	2014
Period	Aug-Jul	Aug-Jul	Aug-Apr	Aug-Apr	Apr
Cyprus	25	81	81	22	22
Egypt	1,064	2,257	2,207	850	600
Iran	0	1	1	0	0
Israel	1,200	3,218	2,993	1,154	43
Jordan	3,154	2,797	2,048	1,729	414
Kuwait	0	13	8	0	0
Lebanon	588	1,256	1,092	779	323
Qatar	0	75	75	0	0
Saudi Arabia	100	899	725	0	0
Syria	108	0	0	0	0
Turkey	2,798	9,122	9,122	0	0
United Arab Emirates	2,600	5,422	3,598	0	0
Total Middle East	11,636	25,140	21,951	4,533	1,403
Algeria	303	1,638	1,638	0	0
Angola	0	200	0	0	0
Equatorial Guinea	0	5	0	0	0
Mauritius	16	0	0	0	0
Morocco	0	2,510	2,460	0	0
South Africa	50	175	150	25	25
Tunisia	125	1,719	1,719	0	0
Total Africa	494	6,247	5,967	25	25
Hong Kong	0	2	2	0	0
India	3,575	1,174	394	1,308	64
Indonesia	550	0	0	0	0
Japan	93	379	214	309	43
Pakistan	4,177	6,739	4,173	926	200
Philippines	50	21	21	0	0
Singapore	0	29	29	16	0
Sri Lanka	43	0	0	0	0
Taiwan	4	0	0	2	0
Vietnam	0	0	0	2	0
Total Asia	8,491	8,346	4,835	2,562	308
Chile	49	699	324	0	0
Colombia	518	1,625	1,288	485	0
Ecuador	191	199	149	25	0
Paraguay	0	25	0	0	0
Peru	161	265	265	355	182
Venezuela	250	546	546	84	84
Total S. America	1,168	3,359	2,573	948	265

Canadian Chickpea Exports April, 2014

(metric tons)

Crop Year	2011-12	2012-13	2012-13	2013-14	2014
Period	Aug-Jul	Aug-Jul	Aug-Apr	Aug-Apr	Apr
Antigua and Barbuda	0	3	1	5	0
Barbados	1	2	2	0	0
Costa Rica	144	37	37	74	0
Cuba	0	13	11	0	0
Dominica	1	0	0	0	0
Dominican Republic	129	600	205	1	0
Guatemala	39	22	22	0	0
Jamaica	2	2	2	0	0
Mexico	90	19	19	0	0
Panama	78	8	5	6	0
Trinidad	1,118	1,213	991	989	201
Total C. America	1,602	1,918	1,295	1,076	201
Total World	38,154	71,633	56,309	26,896	4,916

Source: Statistics Canada

Canadian Kabuli Chickpea Exports April, 2014

(metric tons)

Crop Year	2011-12	2012-13	2012-13	2013-14	2014
Period	Aug-Jul	Aug-Jul	Aug-Apr	Aug-Apr	Apr
Top Five Buyers					
United States	5,239	6,895	4,217	7,658	878
United Kingdom	1,558	3,041	2,039	2,139	456
Jordan	2,389	2,797	2,048	1,664	414
India	731	671	0	1,308	64
Israel	1,100	2,991	2,766	1,154	43
Subtotal	11,017	16,395	11,070	13,923	1,856
Percent of Total	45.0%	27.4%	23.8%	64.4%	44.8%
All Buyers					
United States	5,239	6,895	4,217	7,658	878
Total N. America	5,239	6,895	4,217	7,658	878

Canadian Kabuli Chickpea Exports April, 2014

(metric tons)

Crop Year	2011-12	2012-13	2012-13	2013-14	2014
Period	Aug-Jul	Aug-Jul	Aug-Apr	Aug-Apr	Apr
Belgium	190	317	272	765	145
France	0	43	0	48	0
Germany	60	175	175	40	20
Greece	25	241	218	0	0
Italy	1,262	3,701	3,355	875	275
Netherlands	230	629	604	276	150
Portugal	299	0	0	0	0
Spain	398	3,193	2,751	962	24
Sweden	0	204	50	40	0
Switzerland	48	25	0	45	0
United Kingdom	1,558	3,041	2,039	2,139	456
Total W. Europe	4,070	11,570	9,465	5,190	1,069
Bosnia and Herzegovina	0	25	25	0	0
Bulgaria	0	274	25	0	0
Croatia	0	70	70	25	0
Czech Republic	0	249	249	60	0
Hungary	0	100	0	0	0
Kazakhstan	0	53	53	0	0
Lithuania	0	21	21	0	0
Poland	41	45	20	34	0
Russia	0	75	75	50	0
Total E. Europe	41	913	539	169	0
Cyprus	25	81	81	22	22
Egypt	568	2,042	1,992	850	600
Israel	1,100	2,991	2,766	1,154	43
Jordan	2,389	2,797	2,048	1,664	414
Kuwait	0	13	8	0	0
Lebanon	588	1,190	1,092	775	323
Qatar	0	75	75	0	0
Saudi Arabia	100	799	626	0	0
Syria	108	0	0	0	0
Turkey	1,460	7,601	7,601	0	0
United Arab Emirates	1,565	5,400	3,576	0	0
Total Middle East	7,902	22,989	19,866	4,464	1,403

Canadian Kabuli Chickpea Exports April, 2014

(metric tons)

Crop Year	2011-12	2012-13	2012-13	2013-14	2014
Period	Aug-Jul	Aug-Jul	Aug-Apr	Aug-Apr	Apr
Algeria	174	540	540	0	0
Angola	0	200	0	0	0
Equatorial Guinea	0	5	0	0	0
Mauritius	13	0	0	0	0
Morocco	0	2,510	2,460	0	0
South Africa	50	175	150	25	25
Tunisia	125	1,569	1,569	0	0
Total Africa	362	4,999	4,719	25	25
Hong Kong	0	2	2	0	0
India	731	671	0	1,308	64
Japan	84	379	214	286	43
Pakistan	3,843	6,280	3,816	901	200
Philippines	50	21	21	0	0
Singapore	0	27	27	0	0
Taiwan	0	0	0	2	0
Vietnam	0	0	0	2	0
Total Asia	4,709	7,381	4,081	2,498	308
Chile	49	699	324	0	0
Colombia	427	1,476	1,189	125	0
Ecuador	148	177	127	25	0
Paraguay	0	25	0	0	0
Peru	161	265	265	328	182
Venezuela	0	546	546	84	84
Total S. America	785	3,188	2,451	561	265
Barbados	1	2	2	0	0
Costa Rica	144	37	37	74	0
Cuba	0	2	0	0	0
Dominican Republic	129	600	205	1	0
Guatemala	39	22	22	0	0
Mexico	90	0	0	0	0
Panama	2	8	5	6	0
Trinidad	992	1,209	986	989	200
Total C. America	1,398	1,880	1,258	1,070	200
Total World	24,506	59,815	46,596	21,636	4,148

Source: Statistics Canada

U.S. Chickpea Exports April, 2014

(metric tons)

Crop Year	2011-12	2012-13	2012-13	2013-14	2014
Period	Sep-Aug	Sep-Aug	Sep-Apr	Sep-Apr	Apr
Top Five Buyers					
Spain	21,145	16,446	13,038	12,431	453
Turkey	2,839	8,961	8,335	8,696	232
Italy	4,471	3,415	3,085	2,465	47
India	10,240	7,346	6,675	2,083	853
Lebanon	2,872	1,715	1,437	1,617	117
Subtotal	41,567	37,882	32,569	27,292	1,701
Percent of Total	52.4%	57.6%	56.2%	72.7%	47.6%
All Buyers					
Canada	5,752	4,183	3,051	1,062	180
Total N. America	5,752	4,183	3,051	1,062	180
Belgium	468	327	303	113	93
France	718	0	0	0	0
Germany	48	100	55	28	0
Greece	185	0	0	69	0
Italy	4,471	3,415	3,085	2,465	47
Netherlands	58	14	9	124	3
Norway	73	0	0	0	0
Portugal	1,917	1,762	1,762	1,153	0
Spain	21,145	16,446	13,038	12,431	453
Sweden	110	85	64	22	0
United Kingdom	1,056	501	399	185	0
Total W. Europe	30,248	22,650	18,714	16,589	595
Armenia	54	0	0	23	0
Bosnia and Herzegovina	44	0	0	0	0
Croatia	0	22	0	0	0
Georgia	51	0	0	0	0
Russia	259	258	215	106	42
Ukraine	0	0	0	68	0
Total E. Europe	408	280	215	198	42

U.S. Chickpea Exports April, 2014
(metric tons)

Crop Year	2011-12	2012-13	2012-13	2013-14	2014
Period	Sep-Aug	Sep-Aug	Sep-Apr	Sep-Apr	Apr
Cyprus	0	0	0	23	0
Egypt	0	141	141	0	0
Iran	0	7,144	7,144	0	0
Israel	2,141	1,573	1,551	105	0
Jordan	1,303	92	69	113	23
Lebanon	2,872	1,715	1,437	1,617	117
Qatar	91	23	23	70	0
Saudi Arabia	0	72	72	0	0
Syria	22	0	0	0	0
Turkey	2,839	8,961	8,335	8,696	232
United Arab Emirates	499	712	712	907	68
Total Middle East	9,767	20,433	19,485	11,532	440
Algeria	1,768	2,219	2,103	463	0
South Africa	24	0	0	0	0
Tunisia	373	348	348	0	0
Total Africa	2,165	2,567	2,451	463	0
China	0	134	134	0	0
Hong Kong	160	83	69	52	0
India	10,240	7,346	6,675	2,083	853
Indonesia	297	53	53	0	0
Japan	1,978	1,136	783	475	0
Korea South	11	84	71	0	0
Malaysia	985	45	45	44	0
Pakistan	5,945	1,248	1,248	1,472	1,301
Philippines	1,568	322	322	274	23
Singapore	21	0	0	0	0
Sri Lanka	751	474	474	0	0
Taiwan	324	412	324	369	71
Thailand	62	240	240	0	0
Vietnam	186	150	150	23	18
Total Asia	22,528	11,726	10,586	4,791	2,266
New Zealand	1,429	959	765	252	28
Total Pacific	1,429	959	765	252	28
Colombia	1,560	1,147	1,147	1,391	0
Peru	4,389	986	963	579	0
Suriname	3	9	7	5	0
Venezuela	186	0	0	0	0
Total S. America	6,138	2,142	2,116	1,975	0

U.S. Chickpea Exports April, 2014

(metric tons)

Crop Year	2011-12	2012-13	2012-13	2013-14	2014
Period	Sep-Aug	Sep-Aug	Sep-Apr	Sep-Apr	Apr
Barbados	39	24	17	8	0
Bermuda	42	0	0	0	0
Costa Rica	106	71	71	44	22
Dominican Republic	136	163	145	100	3
Guatemala	3	0	0	27	0
Honduras	10	3	3	3	0
Jamaica	24	4	4	2	0
Mexico	38	454	190	406	0
Netherlands Antilles	2	0	0	0	0
Nicaragua	0	1	1	0	0
Panama	58	28	7	19	0
Trinidad	434	136	113	46	0
Total C. America	891	884	551	655	25
Total World	79,325	65,825	57,935	37,515	3,575

Source: U.S. Department of Commerce

Birdseeds

Canaryseed

Canadian Canaryseed Supply and Demand Estimates
(metric tons, acres)

Year	2010	2011	2012	2013	2014
Acreage	395,000	275,000	335,000	210,000	245,000
Yield (lbs)	857	1,031	985	1,375	1,089
Production	153,500	128,600	149,700	131,000	121,000
Carryin	69,000	30,000	17,000	22,000	5,000
Stocks	222,500	158,600	166,700	153,000	126,000
Disappearance					
Aug-Apr Exports	130,538	96,369	98,114	113,689	N/A
Percent of Forecast	73.0 %	76.3 %	72.0 %	80.4 %	N/A
North Europe	35,631	25,889	23,745	24,800	19,600
Mediterranean	23,870	22,999	20,290	23,100	17,500
Americas	108,804	61,014	78,166	74,600	61,900
Pacific Rim	3,300	4,505	7,725	10,500	6,000
Arab/Africa	7,280	11,978	6,310	8,400	7,000
Total Export	178,884	126,385	136,236	141,400	112,000
All Domestic	13,616	15,214	8,465	6,600	7,000
Usage	192,500	141,599	144,701	148,000	119,000
Carryover	30,000	17,000	22,000	5,000	7,000
Stocks/Use	15.6 %	12.0 %	15.2 %	3.4 %	5.9 %

Forecasts by STAT Market Research based on data from Statistics Canada

Canadian Canaryseed Exports April, 2014

(metric tons)

Crop Year	2011-12	2012-13	2012-13	2013-14	2014
Period	Aug-Jul	Aug-Jul	Aug-Apr	Aug-Apr	Apr
Top Five Buyers					
Mexico	22,665	36,894	27,173	25,221	1,928
Belgium	25,339	22,510	14,861	17,795	166
Brazil	3,482	6,415	4,892	9,571	834
Spain	9,672	9,101	7,060	7,465	1,452
United States	10,559	11,299	7,754	6,930	821
Subtotal	71,717	86,220	61,740	66,981	5,202
Percent of Total	56.7%	63.3%	62.9%	58.9%	38.5%
All Buyers					
United States	10,559	11,299	7,754	6,930	821
Total N. America	10,559	11,299	7,754	6,930	821
Belgium	25,339	22,510	14,861	17,795	166
France	22	92	92	22	0
Germany	73	576	361	721	88
Greece	769	790	632	621	89
Italy	5,354	3,768	2,557	6,126	822
Malta	646	594	572	362	0
Netherlands	112	0	0	281	97
Portugal	4,170	3,824	2,939	2,727	271
Spain	9,672	9,101	7,060	7,465	1,452
Sweden	109	107	86	108	22
United Kingdom	55	68	68	50	0
Total W. Europe	46,320	41,430	29,228	36,276	3,008
Albania	0	0	0	131	0
Bulgaria	22	65	65	43	0
Czech Republic	0	45	0	22	0
Hungary	0	0	0	461	67
Poland	0	0	0	185	138
Russia	158	281	238	177	0
Total E. Europe	180	391	302	1,018	205

Canadian Canaryseed Exports April, 2014
(metric tons)

Crop Year Period	2011-12 Aug-Jul	2012-13 Aug-Jul	2012-13 Aug-Apr	2013-14 Aug-Apr	2014 Apr
Cyprus	88	66	43	43	0
Egypt	1,886	1,340	1,119	1,725	678
Iran	356	0	0	0	0
Israel	399	230	165	519	87
Jordan	617	520	312	644	47
Kuwait	95	47	47	0	0
Lebanon	701	117	93	662	89
Libya	94	139	23	75	4
Saudi Arabia	119	93	71	164	0
Syria	997	385	314	330	0
Turkey	2,301	2,147	1,895	2,533	586
United Arab Emirates	1,445	185	185	1,051	0
Total Middle East	9,099	5,270	4,268	7,747	1,492
Algeria	2,458	980	884	2,618	69
Mauritius	10	13	0	92	0
Morocco	1,054	676	631	582	0
South Africa	242	394	373	193	0
Tunisia	1,504	1,190	1,121	1,725	0
Total Africa	5,268	3,253	3,010	5,210	69
China	0	68	68	0	0
Hong Kong	0	2	2	0	0
India	0	182	182	100	0
Indonesia	2,111	4,064	2,662	6,400	2,568
Japan	931	1,042	643	729	170
Korea South	109	155	131	90	0
Malaysia	10	21	10	0	0
Pakistan	114	268	194	495	0
Philippines	425	398	284	266	24
Taiwan	526	1,044	914	627	163
Thailand	65	66	66	135	68
Vietnam	47	180	180	0	0
Total Asia	4,337	7,491	5,337	8,842	2,992
New Zealand	168	230	167	147	0
U.S. Minor Outlying Islands	0	4	1	6	0
Total Pacific	168	234	168	153	0

Canadian Canaryseed Exports April, 2014
(metric tons)

Crop Year	2011-12	2012-13	2012-13	2013-14	2014
Period	Aug-Jul	Aug-Jul	Aug-Apr	Aug-Apr	Apr
Brazil	3,482	6,415	4,892	9,571	834
Chile	2,598	2,341	1,373	1,560	140
Colombia	8,809	12,303	8,609	4,560	540
Ecuador	1,545	1,157	686	1,153	180
Guyana	15	42	36	32	12
Peru	4,165	3,079	2,069	2,247	571
Suriname	61	80	80	21	0
Uruguay	47	230	68	352	47
Venezuela	4,171	923	776	987	384
Total S. America	24,893	26,570	18,589	20,482	2,709
Costa Rica	602	643	411	372	25
Cuba	245	336	231	128	0
Dominican Republic	494	427	297	505	174
El Salvador	237	407	261	99	25
Guatemala	837	1,150	733	508	44
Honduras	98	66	66	51	23
Mexico	22,665	36,894	27,173	25,221	1,928
Panama	180	94	78	54	0
Trinidad	203	280	210	94	7
Total C. America	25,562	40,297	29,459	27,033	2,226
Total World	126,385	136,236	98,114	113,689	13,522

Source: Statistics Canada

U.S. Canaryseed Exports April, 2014

(metric tons)

Crop Year	2011-12	2012-13	2012-13	2013-14	2014
Period	Sep-Aug	Sep-Aug	Sep-Apr	Sep-Apr	Apr
Bermuda	1	0	0	0	0
Brazil	134	68	68	0	0
Colombia	0	190	190	0	0
Dominican Republic	0	69	69	0	0
Italy	0	379	379	101	0
Japan	314	129	129	0	0
Jordan	22	0	0	0	0
Mexico	38	246	246	0	0
Peru	0	70	0	0	0
Spain	0	149	82	0	0
Taiwan	64	0	0	0	0
Trinidad	14	16	12	0	0
Venezuela	129	0	0	0	0
Total World	714	1,317	1,177	101	0

Source: U.S. Department of Commerce

Australian Canaryseed Exports April, 2014

(metric tons)

Crop Year	2011-12	2012-13	2012-13	2013-14	2014
Period	Nov-Oct	Nov-Oct	Nov-Apr	Nov-Apr	Apr
Bangladesh	2	0	0	0	0
Germany	0	1	0	0	0
Japan	28	12	9	11	0
Kuwait	0	44	0	0	0
Mauritius	0	3	0	0	0
Saudi Arabia	44	0	0	0	0
Taiwan	108	0	0	0	0
Thailand	156	127	44	0	0
Total World	337	186	53	11	0

Source: Australia Bureau of Statistics

Millet

Australian Millet Exports April, 2014
(metric tons)

Crop Year	2011-12	2012-13	2012-13	2013-14	2014
Period	Nov-Oct	Nov-Oct	Nov-Apr	Nov-Apr	Apr
Top Five Buyers					
Japan	20,874	20,820	446	12,169	0
New Zealand	1,071	953	483	341	38
Belgium	518	617	406	128	0
Korea South	33	34	16	25	0
Subtotal	22,497	22,424	1,351	12,664	38
Percent of Total	95.7%	95.6%	81.5%	100.0%	98.1%
All Buyers					
Canada	25	21	21	0	0
Total N. America	25	21	21	0	0
Belgium	518	617	406	128	0
France	40	0	0	0	0
Germany	16	1	0	0	0
Italy	191	202	157	0	0
Netherlands	17	102	0	0	0
Portugal	45	0	0	0	0
United Kingdom	18	53	16	0	0
Total W. Europe	845	975	580	128	0
Israel	0	25	3	0	0
Kuwait	45	23	0	0	0
Lebanon	0	87	0	0	0
Oman	1	0	0	0	0
United Arab Emirates	110	89	0	0	0
Total Middle East	156	224	3	0	0
Mauritius	0	84	0	0	0
South Africa	20	0	0	0	0
Total Africa	20	84	0	0	0

Australian Millet Exports April, 2014
(metric tons)

Crop Year	2011-12	2012-13	2012-13	2013-14	2014
Period	Nov-Oct	Nov-Oct	Nov-Apr	Nov-Apr	Apr
Indonesia	0	153	110	0	0
Japan	20,874	20,820	446	12,169	0
Korea South	33	34	16	25	0
Malaysia	0	66	0	0	0
Philippines	130	0	0	0	0
Sri Lanka	44	0	0	0	0
Thailand	220	136	0	2	1
Total Asia	21,302	21,209	572	12,196	1
New Zealand	1,071	953	483	341	38
Papua New Guinea	97	1	0	0	0
Total Pacific	1,168	955	484	341	38
Total World	23,515	23,468	1,659	12,666	39

Source: Australia Bureau of Statistics

U.S. Millet Exports April, 2014
(metric tons)

Crop Year	2011-12	2012-13	2012-13	2013-14	2014
Period	Sep-Aug	Sep-Aug	Sep-Apr	Sep-Apr	Apr
Top Five Buyers					
Indonesia	10,044	262	262	14,740	1,630
Canada	11,681	4,974	4,290	6,149	814
Malaysia	4,161	63	63	3,766	491
Mexico	5,220	2,419	1,839	3,488	421
Philippines	6,673	0	0	3,229	471
Subtotal	37,779	7,718	6,454	31,372	3,827
Percent of Total	70.0%	66.4%	71.5%	74.2%	61.9%
All Buyers					
Canada	11,681	4,974	4,290	6,149	814
Total N. America	11,681	4,974	4,290	6,149	814
Belgium	1,178	365	263	262	59
Denmark	0	0	0	41	0
Finland	0	0	0	60	20
France	1,906	347	347	134	34
Germany	1,601	811	687	337	81
Greece	20	0	0	0	0
Italy	747	106	85	477	21
Netherlands	1,247	41	41	143	20
Norway	204	0	0	61	0
Portugal	140	0	0	21	21
Switzerland	66	0	0	0	0
United Kingdom	2,094	591	591	1,046	281
Total W. Europe	9,202	2,260	2,014	2,581	537
Poland	0	6	6	0	0
Total E. Europe	0	6	6	0	0
Bahrain	21	0	0	166	83
Egypt	90	0	0	61	61
Israel	506	0	0	345	102
Jordan	466	0	0	593	20
Kuwait	83	0	0	186	41
Lebanon	41	40	0	102	0
Oman	21	0	0	0	0
Saudi Arabia	230	59	59	500	227
Turkey	204	0	0	0	0
United Arab Emirates	847	0	0	806	208
Total Middle East	2,508	99	59	2,758	743

U.S. Millet Exports April, 2014

(metric tons)

Crop Year	2011-12	2012-13	2012-13	2013-14	2014
Period	Sep-Aug	Sep-Aug	Sep-Apr	Sep-Apr	Apr
Cameroon	0	1,002	0	0	0
Djibouti	477	0	0	0	0
South Africa	91	0	0	20	20
Total Africa	568	1,002	0	20	20
China	0	0	0	37	1
Hong Kong	0	0	0	8	0
Indonesia	10,044	262	262	14,740	1,630
Japan	888	24	8	753	146
Korea South	0	0	0	535	20
Malaysia	4,161	63	63	3,766	491
Philippines	6,673	0	0	3,229	471
Singapore	41	0	0	21	0
Sri Lanka	83	0	0	152	90
Taiwan	455	22	22	561	20
Thailand	565	60	60	1,781	492
Total Asia	22,910	431	415	25,582	3,361
Australia	0	0	0	505	162
New Zealand	121	0	0	184	41
Total Pacific	121	0	0	688	203
Brazil	0	0	0	20	0
Chile	20	0	0	20	0
Colombia	53	0	0	326	41
Peru	166	0	0	0	0
Total S. America	239	0	0	366	41
Cayman Islands	31	165	138	78	0
Costa Rica	427	41	41	123	0
Dominican Republic	0	0	0	20	0
El Salvador	568	141	141	121	0
Guatemala	370	81	81	191	21
Honduras	103	0	0	82	21
Mexico	5,220	2,419	1,839	3,488	421
Panama	0	0	0	20	0
Trinidad	6	0	0	4	0
Total C. America	6,724	2,847	2,239	4,126	463
Total World	53,953	11,618	9,023	42,270	6,180

Source: U.S. Department of Commerce

Oilseed

Sunflower Seed

Canadian Sunflower Seed Supply and Demand Estimates
(metric tons, acres)

Year	2010	2011	2012	2013	2014
Acreage	135,000	35,000	100,000	70,000	125,000
Yield (pounds)	1,104	1,247	1,916	1,635	1,464
Production (MT)	67,600	19,800	86,900	51,900	83,000
Imports	26,000	24,800	18,200	21,200	21,700
Carryin	42,000	36,000	7,000	19,300	4,777
Stocks	135,600	80,600	112,100	92,400	109,477
Disappearance					
Aug-Mar Exports	31,914	22,926	25,531	32,859	N/A
Percent of Forecast	69.8 %	68.8 %	58.4 %	64.4 %	N/A
Export	45,704	33,343	43,752	51,000	52,000
Seed & Waste	3,808	1,719	4,698	3,383	4,399
Domestic	50,088	38,539	44,349	33,241	41,718
Usage	99,600	73,601	92,799	87,624	98,117
Carryover	36,000	7,000	19,300	4,777	11,360
Usage/Stocks	36.1 %	9.5 %	20.8 %	5.5 %	11.6 %

Forecasts by STAT Market Research based on data from Statistics Canada

Canadian Sunflower Seed Exports April, 2014

(metric tons)

Crop Year	2011-12	2012-13	2012-13	2013-14	2014
Period	Aug-Jul	Aug-Jul	Aug-Apr	Aug-Apr	Apr
Top Five Buyers					
United States	27,731	35,135	26,478	30,683	4,282
Turkey	0	2,368	1,263	1,094	427
Mexico	1,488	759	375	889	113
United Arab Emirates	209	651	179	821	62
Syria	1,016	450	337	809	0
Subtotal	30,445	39,363	28,632	34,296	4,883
Percent of Total	91.3%	90.0%	91.0%	90.4%	96.2%
All Buyers					
United States	27,731	35,135	26,478	30,683	4,282
Total N. America	27,731	35,135	26,478	30,683	4,282
France	0	0	0	1	0
Portugal	0	0	0	36	0
Spain	20	111	111	0	0
Total W. Europe	20	111	111	37	0
Egypt	124	410	207	458	0
Iran	39	0	0	0	0
Iraq	60	61	0	313	0
Jordan	286	260	150	0	0
Kuwait	126	404	233	565	0
Lebanon	253	383	197	118	0
Libya	22	0	0	0	0
Saudi Arabia	0	160	88	47	0
Syria	1,016	450	337	809	0
Turkey	0	2,368	1,263	1,094	427
United Arab Emirates	209	651	179	821	62
Total Middle East	2,137	5,145	2,653	4,225	489
Mauritius	6	0	0	0	0
South Africa	25	6	6	26	0
Tunisia	513	404	264	271	0
Total Africa	544	410	270	297	0
Hong Kong	6	8	8	10	0
Indonesia	69	64	44	27	0
Japan	376	547	422	263	24
Korea South	0	0	0	22	22
Malaysia	5	52	16	162	45
Philippines	0	0	0	24	0
Taiwan	0	20	0	0	0
Vietnam	0	48	0	0	0
Total Asia	456	738	490	508	91

Canadian Sunflower Seed Exports April, 2014
(metric tons)

Crop Year	2011-12	2012-13	2012-13	2013-14	2014
Period	Aug-Jul	Aug-Jul	Aug-Apr	Aug-Apr	Apr
Australia	0	1	1	2	1
U.S. Minor Outlying Islands	45	31	31	25	0
Total Pacific	45	32	32	27	1
Chile	181	234	197	505	0
Colombia	66	25	25	0	0
Guyana	0	5	5	12	7
Suriname	67	109	85	11	0
Venezuela	0	74	74	22	0
Total S. America	314	448	386	550	7
	0	0	0	2	2
Aruba	0	22	22	0	0
Costa Rica	376	598	431	467	79
Cuba	45	150	85	68	0
Dominican Republic	6	12	10	39	0
Guatemala	17	22	22	30	0
Honduras	35	50	29	0	0
Jamaica	2	3	3	0	0
Mexico	1,488	759	375	889	113
Netherlands Antilles	0	8	6	6	0
Panama	52	48	24	36	0
Trinidad	75	60	47	75	15
Total C. America	2,097	1,733	1,055	1,611	209
Total World	33,343	43,752	31,476	37,938	5,078

Source: Statistics Canada

U.S. Oil Sunflower Seed Exports April, 2014

(metric tons)

Crop Year	2011-12	2012-13	2012-13	2013-14	2014
Period	Sep-Aug	Sep-Aug	Sep-Apr	Sep-Apr	Apr
Top Five Buyers					
Canada	24,517	22,193	16,180	12,557	1,255
France	2,716	4,929	4,915	3,694	1
Mexico	2,251	3,498	1,974	1,687	336
China	1,839	2,387	2,336	1,309	90
Turkey	16	0	0	753	1
Subtotal	31,339	33,006	25,405	19,999	1,684
Percent of Total	77.1%	81.7%	79.8%	94.6%	90.1%
All Buyers					
Canada	24,517	22,193	16,180	12,557	1,255
Total N. America	24,517	22,193	16,180	12,557	1,255
Austria	2,131	1,503	1,503	0	0
Belgium	0	369	369	0	0
France	2,716	4,929	4,915	3,694	1
Germany	2,310	1,354	1,354	0	0
Italy	181	131	131	0	0
Norway	1	0	0	0	0
Spain	183	0	0	0	0
Switzerland	0	5	0	0	0
Total W. Europe	7,521	8,290	8,272	3,694	1
Bulgaria	0	141	141	0	0
Croatia	53	0	0	0	0
Hungary	808	934	934	0	0
Romania	1,421	1,050	1,050	20	20
Russia	1,011	161	161	363	0
Ukraine	614	38	38	0	0
Total E. Europe	3,906	2,324	2,324	383	20
Egypt	0	191	0	0	0
Israel	2	666	142	156	19
Jordan	0	61	61	0	0
Kuwait	0	4	0	0	0
Turkey	16	0	0	753	1
United Arab Emirates	0	1	1	0	0
Total Middle East	19	922	203	909	20

U.S. Oil Sunflower Seed Exports April, 2014

(metric tons)

Crop Year	2011-12	2012-13	2012-13	2013-14	2014
Period	Sep-Aug	Sep-Aug	Sep-Apr	Sep-Apr	Apr
China	1,839	2,387	2,336	1,309	90
Japan	302	182	112	369	47
Korea South	54	190	154	134	98
Malaysia	0	85	7	0	0
Pakistan	0	183	183	0	0
Philippines	20	0	0	0	0
Taiwan	41	0	0	0	0
Thailand	0	3	3	0	0
Total Asia	2,256	3,030	2,795	1,812	235
Australia	12	0	0	0	0
Total Pacific	12	0	0	0	0
Argentina	51	48	0	12	0
Brazil	67	0	0	0	0
Chile	6	27	27	0	0
Colombia	1	0	0	0	0
Ecuador	10	0	0	0	0
Total S. America	134	75	27	12	0
Costa Rica	11	0	0	10	0
El Salvador	2	0	0	0	0
Guatemala	0	47	47	67	0
Mexico	2,251	3,498	1,974	1,687	336
Trinidad	3	2	2	0	0
Total C. America	2,268	3,546	2,023	1,764	336
Total World	40,632	40,381	31,824	21,130	1,868

Source: U.S. Department of Commerce

Australian Sunflower Seed Exports April, 2014

(metric tons)

Crop Year	2011-12	2012-13	2012-13	2013-14	2014
Period	Nov-Oct	Nov-Oct	Nov-Apr	Nov-Apr	Apr
Top Five Buyers					
New Caledonia	146	234	134	90	0
New Zealand	156	237	142	67	0
Japan	50	134	85	39	0
Philippines	398	25	0	28	0
Subtotal	750	630	361	224	0
Percent of Total	79.1%	86.9%	89.4%	95.4%	0.0%
All Buyers					
France	1	0	0	0	0
Total W. Europe	1	0	0	0	0
Lebanon	0	13	0	0	0
Sudan	66	0	0	0	0
Total Middle East	66	13	0	0	0
South Africa	0	2	0	0	0
Total Africa	0	2	0	0	0
China	0	4	4	0	0
Hong Kong	23	16	7	8	2
Japan	50	134	85	39	0
Pakistan	13	0	0	0	0
Philippines	398	25	0	28	0
Thailand	96	59	31	3	3
Total Asia	580	239	127	78	5
French Polynesia	0	1	1	0	0
New Caledonia	146	234	134	90	0
New Zealand	156	237	142	67	0
Total Pacific	302	471	276	157	0
Total World	948	725	404	235	5

Source: Australia Bureau of Statistics

Safflower

Canadian Safflower Seed Exports April, 2014
(metric tons)

Crop Year	2011-12	2012-13	2012-13	2013-14	2014
Period	Aug-Jul	Aug-Jul	Aug-Apr	Aug-Apr	Apr
Colombia	16	26	26	0	0
Costa Rica	2	0	0	3	0
Guatemala	4	0	0	0	0
Hong Kong	3	0	0	0	0
Indonesia	0	7	5	0	0
Netherlands Antilles	0	1	1	0	0
Trinidad	0	1	1	2	0
U.S. Minor Outlying Islands	0	68	1	0	0
United States	147	467	314	277	15
Total World	173	570	348	282	15

Source: Statistics Canada

Australian Safflower Seed Exports April, 2014
(metric tons)

Crop Year	2011-12	2012-13	2012-13	2013-14	2014
Period	Nov-Oct	Nov-Oct	Nov-Apr	Nov-Apr	Apr
Bahrain	225	34	34	0	0
Belgium	55	0	0	0	0
India	0	0	0	32	0
Japan	189	316	182	0	0
Korea South	0	0	0	11	0
New Zealand	18	0	0	0	0
Philippines	462	528	432	0	0
South Africa	33	33	0	0	0
Sri Lanka	33	0	0	0	0
Taiwan	1,455	368	300	324	162
United Kingdom	213	331	226	0	0
Vietnam	0	60	60	0	0
Total World	2,682	1,669	1,233	367	162

Source: Australia Bureau of Statistics

Canola and Rapeseed

Canadian Canola Exports April, 2014
(metric tons)

Crop Year	2011-12	2012-13	2012-13	2013-14	2014
Period	Aug-Jul	Aug-Jul	Aug-Apr	Aug-Apr	Apr
Top Five Buyers					
China	2,525,292	2,670,420	2,391,018	2,953,081	475,618
Japan	2,315,065	2,318,164	1,726,106	1,565,839	202,256
Mexico	1,504,710	1,390,954	1,135,875	984,840	125,262
United States	579,433	416,777	335,612	766,040	114,268
United Arab Emirates	686,621	232,612	232,612	215,749	57,800
Subtotal	7,611,121	7,028,928	5,821,223	6,485,548	975,203
Percent of Total	87.5%	98.8%	98.6%	99.6%	99.9%
All Buyers					
United States	579,433	416,777	335,612	766,040	114,268
Total N. America	579,433	416,777	335,612	766,040	114,268
Belgium	81,969	0	0	0	0
France	57,900	0	0	0	0
Italy	0	23	23	0	0
Portugal	74,115	43,591	43,591	25	0
Spain	25	0	0	0	0
Total W. Europe	214,008	43,614	43,614	25	0
Israel	44	0	0	0	0
Lebanon	78	23	23	24	0
Turkey	152	0	0	4	0
United Arab Emirates	686,621	232,612	232,612	215,749	57,800
Total Middle East	686,894	232,635	232,635	215,777	57,800

Canadian Canola Exports April, 2014
(metric tons)

Crop Year	2011-12	2012-13	2012-13	2013-14	2014
Period	Aug-Jul	Aug-Jul	Aug-Apr	Aug-Apr	Apr
Bangladesh	244,335	10,000	10,000	2	0
China	2,525,292	2,670,420	2,391,018	2,953,081	475,618
Hong Kong	138	550	386	352	111
India	0	0	0	614	0
Indonesia	113	295	216	558	136
Japan	2,315,065	2,318,164	1,726,106	1,565,839	202,256
Korea South	0	28,953	28,953	0	0
Nepal	1,965	0	0	0	0
Pakistan	622,018	0	0	20,793	0
Taiwan	51	161	161	101	101
Vietnam	388	607	607	1,608	548
Total Asia	5,709,365	5,029,150	4,157,446	4,542,947	678,769
Australia	326	147	147	6	6
Total Pacific	326	147	147	6	6
Chile	29	10	10	4	0
Colombia	183	436	278	148	43
Venezuela	117	0	0	0	0
Total S. America	328	446	288	152	43
Costa Rica	86	73	32	67	0
Guatemala	28	76	76	0	0
Mexico	1,504,710	1,390,954	1,135,875	984,840	125,262
Trinidad	2	0	0	0	0
Total C. America	1,504,825	1,391,104	1,135,983	984,907	125,262
Total World	8,695,179	7,113,875	5,905,727	6,509,853	976,148

Source: Statistics Canada

Australian Rapeseed Exports April, 2014
(metric tons)

Crop Year	2011-12	2012-13	2012-13	2013-14	2014
Period	Nov-Oct	Nov-Oct	Nov-Apr	Nov-Apr	Apr
Belgium	3,836	368	170	388	65
India	0	42	42	0	0
Indonesia	1	40	0	0	0
Italy	21	0	0	19	0
Japan	5,018	6,522	2,474	4,364	401
Kuwait	0	20	20	20	0
Malaysia	603	3,412	3,412	4,875	0
Nepal	2,022	457	457	0	0
Netherlands	235	129	107	87	0
New Zealand	0	241	0	0	0
Pakistan	0	0	0	8,691	759
Papua New Guinea	0	39	0	0	0
Philippines	0	0	0	5	0
South Africa	29	33	33	838	15
Spain	0	0	0	43	21
Vietnam	0	32,938	12,803	29,744	975
Total World	11,765	44,241	19,518	49,077	2,235

Source: Australia Bureau of Statistics

Flaxseed

Canadian Linseed (flax) Exports April, 2014

(metric tons)

Crop Year	2011-12	2012-13	2012-13	2013-14	2014
Period	Aug-Jul	Aug-Jul	Aug-Apr	Aug-Apr	Apr
Top Five Buyers					
China	155,095	158,331	113,969	169,438	7,760
United States	192,626	168,235	126,657	124,257	10,179
Belgium	18,555	113,044	71,446	88,714	25,540
Japan	4,887	5,486	4,688	5,111	2,110
Vietnam	621	10,009	7,968	4,959	1,410
Subtotal	371,784	455,105	324,730	392,479	46,999
Percent of Total	95.2%	94.5%	95.0%	94.6%	94.3%
All Buyers					
United States	192,626	168,235	126,657	124,257	10,179
Total N. America	192,626	168,235	126,658	124,257	10,179
Belgium	18,555	113,044	71,446	88,714	25,540
Denmark	370	200	160	20	0
Finland	0	20	20	119	26
France	26	26	26	0	0
Germany	268	868	717	179	20
Greece	5	54	54	43	0
Ireland	481	155	106	435	0
Italy	73	0	0	50	45
Malta	0	48	48	0	0
Netherlands	183	1,838	1,147	1,194	140
Norway	312	177	104	210	26
Portugal	0	20	20	64	0
Spain	177	251	208	333	21
Sweden	207	363	289	191	48
Switzerland	2	0	0	0	0
United Kingdom	804	1,373	835	1,093	244
Total W. Europe	21,465	118,437	75,181	92,644	26,109

Canadian Linseed (flax) Exports April, 2014
(metric tons)

Crop Year	2011-12	2012-13	2012-13	2013-14	2014
Period	Aug-Jul	Aug-Jul	Aug-Apr	Aug-Apr	Apr
Bulgaria	0	22	22	22	0
Croatia	46	84	42	43	0
Czech Republic	0	64	0	0	0
Hungary	0	6	6	0	0
Poland	0	1,497	882	1,810	177
Russia	22	45	45	68	0
Total E. Europe	68	1,718	996	1,942	177
Bahrain	0	0	0	3	0
Egypt	989	834	834	0	0
Iran	0	431	431	0	0
Israel	648	664	482	781	111
Jordan	12	151	151	0	0
Lebanon	38	27	5	65	0
Saudi Arabia	22	0	0	0	0
Syria	23	0	0	0	0
Turkey	309	42	42	269	0
United Arab Emirates	166	0	0	311	0
Total Middle East	2,207	2,149	1,945	1,428	111
Algeria	0	0	0	24	0
Mauritius	6	0	0	2	0
Morocco	347	1,070	282	565	210
Nigeria	0	4	0	0	0
South Africa	982	1,249	905	483	103
Tunisia	0	0	0	45	0
Total Africa	1,335	2,323	1,187	1,119	313
China	155,095	158,331	113,969	169,438	7,760
Hong Kong	116	57	45	24	1
India	0	5	0	37	0
Indonesia	82	124	67	14	0
Japan	4,887	5,486	4,688	5,111	2,110
Korea South	465	605	330	567	50
Philippines	96	45	45	127	0
Singapore	217	32	30	50	1
Taiwan	1,010	1,471	1,001	1,512	147
Thailand	85	109	86	116	26
Vietnam	621	10,009	7,968	4,959	1,410
Total Asia	162,675	176,275	128,232	181,955	11,505

Canadian Linseed (flax) Exports April, 2014

(metric tons)

Crop Year	2011-12	2012-13	2012-13	2013-14	2014
Period	Aug-Jul	Aug-Jul	Aug-Apr	Aug-Apr	Apr
Australia	954	121	115	33	27
Christmas Island	0	0	0	254	0
New Zealand	0	21	21	0	0
Total Pacific	954	142	136	288	27
Argentina	0	0	0	20	0
Bolivia	0	23	23	60	60
Brazil	24	2,114	1,178	910	67
Chile	367	789	539	642	41
Colombia	1,515	1,169	809	1,494	384
Ecuador	624	682	382	696	67
Peru	1,042	1,233	917	1,539	91
Uruguay	0	161	71	21	0
Venezuela	724	726	259	785	0
Total S. America	4,296	6,896	4,179	6,167	710
Barbados	8	5	5	11	0
Costa Rica	529	426	237	325	21
Dominican Republic	58	73	52	122	27
El Salvador	43	88	66	44	0
Guatemala	159	280	235	157	22
Honduras	0	126	81	41	0
Jamaica	14	1	1	0	0
Mexico	3,894	4,177	2,355	4,104	636
Nicaragua	70	152	108	119	23
Panama	12	11	5	11	0
Trinidad	49	22	16	40	0
Total C. America	4,836	5,361	3,161	4,973	729
Total World	390,462	481,537	341,673	414,773	49,860

Source: Statistics Canada

Soybean

Canadian Soybean Exports April, 2014
(metric tons)

Crop Year	2011-12	2012-13	2012-13	2013-14	2014
Period	Aug-Jul	Aug-Jul	Aug-Apr	Aug-Apr	Apr
Top Five Buyers					
China	189,147	889,401	888,327	722,564	749
United States	502,156	493,914	299,548	478,324	49,289
Netherlands	953,548	488,240	484,478	405,220	735
Japan	487,618	382,329	270,783	268,651	33,144
Belgium	286,808	67,003	63,264	216,137	2,631
Subtotal	2,419,277	2,320,887	2,006,401	2,090,896	86,548
Percent of Total	66.8%	66.9%	65.1%	72.8%	73.6%
All Buyers					
United States	502,156	493,914	299,548	478,324	49,289
Total N. America	502,156	493,914	299,548	478,324	49,289
Austria	41	21	21	16	0
Belgium	286,808	67,003	63,264	216,137	2,631
Denmark	84,383	9,962	9,841	370	0
Finland	0	0	0	21	0
France	79,606	98,606	98,321	1,032	83
Germany	197,916	181,846	160,331	196,934	428
Ireland	181	431	100	4,472	21
Italy	52,744	103,509	102,757	134,328	122
Netherlands	953,548	488,240	484,478	405,220	735
Norway	88,980	83,218	83,218	50,192	0
Portugal	15,279	20	20	21	0
Spain	88,535	111,285	109,823	2,287	260
United Kingdom	300	552	372	0	0
Total W. Europe	1,848,320	1,144,693	1,112,545	1,011,029	4,279

Canadian Soybean Exports April, 2014

(metric tons)

Crop Year	2011-12	2012-13	2012-13	2013-14	2014
Period	Aug-Jul	Aug-Jul	Aug-Apr	Aug-Apr	Apr
Bulgaria	61	120	120	0	0
Croatia	43	0	0	0	0
Czech Republic	122	101	101	0	0
Estonia	0	21	21	0	0
Latvia	0	0	0	52	0
Lithuania	82	81	60	20	0
Poland	917	875	652	734	61
Romania	82	20	20	0	0
Russia	932	180	180	2,795	0
Slovakia	82	20	20	4	4
Ukraine	296	1,160	1,160	2,732	0
Total E. Europe	2,617	2,578	2,334	6,337	65
Egypt	84,285	211,761	211,761	70,011	0
Iran	68,252	37,977	37,977	0	0
Israel	2,046	7,887	7,514	1,566	256
Lebanon	3	75	75	0	0
Saudi Arabia	1,565	30,610	30,368	929	157
Turkey	16,258	32,300	32,300	19,358	0
United Arab Emirates	0	62	21	13,769	20
Total Middle East	172,410	320,671	320,016	105,633	433
Algeria	0	79	79	0	0
Angola	0	30	30	0	0
Mauritius	204	204	163	122	0
Morocco	158	218	39	60	0
Tunisia	0	25,038	25,038	0	0
Total Africa	362	25,569	25,349	182	0
Bangladesh	89	0	0	52,500	0
Brunei Darussalam	163	265	122	469	41
China	189,147	889,401	888,327	722,564	749
Hong Kong	34,224	26,184	20,376	20,462	2,376
Indonesia	12,660	4,523	2,193	31,858	9,369
Japan	487,618	382,329	270,783	268,651	33,144
Korea North	360	0	0	0	0
Korea South	15,188	19,793	19,085	9,286	100
Malaysia	86,603	67,195	52,659	59,727	7,559
Philippines	11,316	6,673	4,750	7,653	1,115
Singapore	22,076	15,015	12,016	12,988	1,485
Taiwan	10,244	8,547	7,066	13,693	1,381
Thailand	50,153	38,240	31,920	29,926	2,359
Vietnam	173,097	23,112	11,703	40,169	3,667
Total Asia	1,092,938	1,481,276	1,321,001	1,269,945	63,344

Canadian Soybean Exports April, 2014

(metric tons)

Crop Year	2011-12	2012-13	2012-13	2013-14	2014
Period	Aug-Jul	Aug-Jul	Aug-Apr	Aug-Apr	Apr
Australia	0	40	40	0	0
New Zealand	881	742	541	699	80
Total Pacific	881	782	581	699	80
Brazil	0	100	100	0	0
Chile	4	8	8	5	0
Guyana	0	4	4	0	0
Peru	1,319	90	90	0	0
Suriname	139	141	81	121	40
Total S. America	1,462	343	283	126	40
Cuba	0	2	2	0	0
Haiti	52	0	0	0	0
Jamaica	1,006	427	331	258	0
Panama	119	125	80	48	15
Trinidad	58	36	36	19	0
Total C. America	1,236	590	449	325	15
Total World	3,622,382	3,470,417	3,082,106	2,872,600	117,546

Source: Statistics Canada

Australian Soybean Exports April, 2014

(metric tons)

Crop Year	2011-12	2012-13	2012-13	2013-14	2014
Period	Nov-Oct	Nov-Oct	Nov-Apr	Nov-Apr	Apr
Fiji	5	0	0	40	0
Korea South	449	5,455	667	62	0
Malaysia	5	1,332	1	238	42
New Caledonia	8	0	0	0	0
New Zealand	1	40	20	0	0
Papua New Guinea	234	243	121	80	0
Taiwan	989	1,249	667	1,144	0
Total World	1,692	8,319	1,476	1,564	42

Source: Australia Bureau of Statistics

Summaries

Canada – Canola Export Quality Summary – April 2014

Dockage (per cent)	2010	2011	2012	2013	April
No 1	1.89	1.84	1.99	1.92	1.97
No 1 NCC	3.12	3.25	3.28	2.91	N/A
Moisture (per cent)	2010	2011	2012	2013	April
No 1	7.68	7.07	6.88	7.22	7.03
No 1 NCC	7.90	7.44	6.87	7.98	N/A
Oil (per cent)	2010	2011	2012	2013	April
No 1	43.56	44.37	43.19	43.85	43.95
No 1 NCC	43.27	43.93	42.66	42.89	N/A
Protein (8.5% moisture)	2010	2011	2012	2013	April
No 1	20.14	19.63	20.94	19.96	19.80
No 1 NCC	19.49	19.62	21.11	20.37	N/A
Protein (oil-free 8.5% moisture)	2010	2011	2012	2013	April
No 1	38.45	38.10	39.30	38.36	38.10
No 1 NCC	38.62	37.77	36.55	38.36	N/A
Chlorophyll (mg/kg)	2010	2011	2012	2013	April
No 1	24.83	23.59	23.52	16.27	14.63
No 1 NCC	22.96	25.19	25.69	14.33	N/A
Oleic Acid (per cent)	2010	2011	2012	2013	April
No 1	61.47	62.44	62.39	63.33	63.92
No 1 NCC	61.73	61.75	62.12	63.15	N/A
Glucosinolates (umol/gram)	2010	2011	2012	2013	April
No 1	12.96	13.06	13.73	12.40	12.54
No 1 NCC	12.25	13.66	14.13	13.11	N/A

Canada – Canola Export Quality Summary – April 2014

Erucic Acid (per cent)	2010	2011	2012	2013	April
No 1	0.03	0.02	0.03	0.02	0.02
No 1 NCC	0.01	0.02	0.03	0.02	N/A
Linolenic Acid (% c18:3)	2010	2011	2012	2013	April
No 1	10.41	10.15	9.69	9.15	8.89
No 1 NCC	10.02	10.16	9.84	9.12	N/A
Saturated Acids (% cn:0)	2010	2011	2012	2013	April
No 1	6.78	6.80	6.63	6.75	6.72
No 1 NCC	6.73	6.81	6.60	6.86	N/A
Iodine Value	2010	2011	2012	2013	April
No 1	114.61	114.05	113.40	111.82	111.21
No 1 NCC	113.80	114.12	113.79	111.74	N/A
Free Fatty Acids (% c18:3)	2010	2011	2012	2013	April
No 1	0.33	0.27	0.32	0.27	0.27
No 1 NCC	0.40	0.34	0.40	0.24	N/A
Cargoes Represented	2010	2011	2012	2013	April
No 1	174	194	168	140	22
No 1 NCC	25	36	48	12	N/A
Metric Tons	2010	2011	2012	2013	April
No 1	5,466,966	6,998,591	5,080,795	5,124,220	863,895
No 1 NCC	694,016	1,130,507	1,790,335	343,707	N/A

SOURCE: Canadian Grain Commission

United States – Minor Oilseed Production Summary

(metric tons, acres, pounds per acre)

Production (metric tons)	2010	2011	2012	2013	2014
Mustard	18,988	7,096	13,576	16,659	14,200
Safflower	100,397	76,962	81,386	95,011	80,200
Canola	1,111,742	697,637	1,110,138	1,002,678	1,234,400
Rapeseed	1,887	1,284	2,214	880	1,600
Flaxseed	230,030	70,890	145,020	85,250	162,800
Oil Sunflower	940,987	781,400	1,088,592	746,986	817,400
Conf. Sunflower	299,859	143,155	174,991	175,052	202,500
Area (Acres)	2010	2011	2012	2013	2014
Mustard	50,500	23,200	51,100	45,000	40,000
Safflower	175,000	130,700	169,800	175,500	143,000
Canola	1,448,800	1,071,500	1,765,000	1,348,000	1,737,000
Rapeseed	2,300	1,500	2,300	1,700	2,000
Flaxseed	421,000	178,000	344,000	181,000	326,000
Oil Sunflower	1,463,000	1,233,400	1,658,000	1,279,000	1,267,000
Conf. Sunflower	488,500	224,400	261,000	296,500	325,000
Yield (pounds)	2010	2011	2012	2013	2014
Mustard	829	674	586	816	783
Safflower	1,265	1,298	1,057	1,194	1,236
Canola	1,692	1,435	1,387	1,640	1,567
Rapeseed	1,809	1,887	2,122	1,141	1,764
Flaxseed	1,205	878	929	1,038	1,101
Oil Sunflower	1,418	1,397	1,447	1,288	1,422
Conf. Sunflower	1,353	1,406	1,478	1,302	1,374

BASED on USDA data. 2013 production forecasts sunflower area breakdown by STAT Publishing

Foods and Spices

Mustard Seed

Canadian Mustard Seed Supply and Demand Estimates
(metric tons, acres)

Year	2010	2011	2012	2013	2014
Acreage	470,000	327,958	335,000	365,000	480,000
Yield	854	874	780	933	868
Production	182,000	130,000	118,600	154,500	189,000
Carryin	82,000	116,000	83,000	36,000	12,000
Stocks	264,000	246,000	201,600	190,500	201,000
Disappearance					
Aug-Dec Exports	84,953	84,773	90,036	101,024	N/A
Percent of Forecast	68.7 %	73.6 %	75.0 %	75.6 %	N/A
Europe	37,211	33,809	44,171	55,200	46,100
Americas	70,974	66,442	63,902	65,500	67,900
Pacific Rim	12,522	12,390	9,419	10,300	11,100
Arab/Africa	2,944	2,544	2,615	2,700	2,700
Total Export	123,651	115,186	120,108	133,700	127,800
Seed/Waste/Other	14,344	16,763	13,118	14,400	18,800
Domestic	10,005	31,051	32,373	30,400	30,400
Usage	148,000	163,000	165,599	178,500	177,000
Carryover	116,000	83,000	36,000	12,000	24,000
Stocks/Use	78.4 %	50.9 %	21.7 %	6.7 %	13.6 %

Forecasts by STAT Market Research based on data from Statistics Canada

Canadian Mustard Seed Exports April, 2014
(metric tons)

Crop Year	2011-12	2012-13	2012-13	2013-14	2014
Period	Aug-Jul	Aug-Jul	Aug-Apr	Aug-Apr	Apr
Top Five Buyers					
United States	61,716	59,414	46,533	44,640	5,080
Germany	7,918	14,458	10,115	13,916	1,033
Belgium	19,357	13,931	10,316	13,083	1,133
Netherlands	2,608	7,693	5,301	5,109	1,131
France	690	3,164	1,713	4,686	1,012
Subtotal	92,289	98,660	73,979	81,434	9,389
Percent of Total	80.1%	82.1%	82.2%	80.6%	79.4%
All Buyers					
United States	61,716	59,414	46,533	44,640	5,080
Total N. America	61,716	59,414	46,533	44,640	5,080
Austria	0	80	40	80	0
Belgium	19,357	13,931	10,316	13,083	1,133
Denmark	7	11	11	7	0
Finland	330	359	260	326	20
France	690	3,164	1,713	4,686	1,012
Germany	7,918	14,458	10,115	13,916	1,033
Greece	351	648	602	810	83
Ireland	1	14	14	0	0
Italy	60	500	480	227	0
Netherlands	2,608	7,693	5,301	5,109	1,131
Spain	27	27	27	88	4
Sweden	24	21	21	111	20
Switzerland	1,437	1,195	888	2,132	224
United Kingdom	716	745	605	392	21
Total W. Europe	33,526	42,846	30,392	40,966	4,681
Croatia	80	118	98	160	20
Czech Republic	0	0	0	168	84
Latvia	22	7	0	0	0
Poland	0	913	746	1,322	84
Romania	0	119	119	177	0
Serbia	0	0	0	42	21
Total E. Europe	101	1,157	963	1,869	209
Israel	1	1	1	0	0
Lebanon	116	69	69	0	0
Turkey	182	168	48	159	65
United Arab Emirates	150	0	0	0	0
Total Middle East	448	238	118	159	65

Canadian Mustard Seed Exports April, 2014

(metric tons)

Crop Year	2011-12	2012-13	2012-13	2013-14	2014
Period	Aug-Jul	Aug-Jul	Aug-Apr	Aug-Apr	Apr
Algeria	22	65	21	71	0
Cote D'ivoire	0	0	0	23	0
Morocco	174	382	340	345	0
Senegal	1,706	1,822	1,134	1,526	128
South Africa	325	251	231	87	0
Total Africa	2,228	2,520	1,726	2,051	128
China	26	31	20	342	99
India	310	20	20	412	174
Japan	5,247	5,467	3,683	3,900	635
Korea South	2,010	1,387	919	710	135
Philippines	168	96	96	156	0
Sri Lanka	0	664	413	168	82
Taiwan	60	80	80	100	0
Thailand	3,688	718	528	1,169	96
Total Asia	11,509	8,463	5,760	6,957	1,221
Australia	881	957	747	648	76
Total Pacific	881	957	747	648	76
Argentina	45	0	0	20	0
Bolivia	0	554	530	317	22
Brazil	896	754	639	784	67
Chile	477	45	45	80	34
Colombia	25	48	48	0	0
Ecuador	486	295	255	399	153
Peru	597	365	262	483	22
Suriname	21	44	44	25	25
Venezuela	1,561	1,925	1,540	1,220	0
Total S. America	4,108	4,029	3,363	3,327	324
Costa Rica	46	30	20	32	0
Dominican Republic	10	0	0	0	0
El Salvador	114	95	76	114	19
Guatemala	337	291	269	240	21
Jamaica	0	20	20	0	0
Mexico	68	0	0	0	0
Panama	50	25	25	0	0
Trinidad	44	24	24	24	0
Total C. America	668	484	434	410	40
Total World	115,186	120,108	90,036	101,027	11,824

Source: Statistics Canada

U.S. Mustard Seed Exports April, 2014
(metric tons)

Crop Year	2011-12	2012-13	2012-13	2013-14	2014
Period	Sep-Aug	Sep-Aug	Sep-Apr	Sep-Apr	Apr
Top Five Buyers					
Canada	335	1,211	637	835	231
Mexico	224	101	101	368	87
Thailand	321	0	0	300	0
New Zealand	7	64	23	249	0
Hong Kong	24	0	0	186	0
Subtotal	910	1,376	761	1,939	318
Percent of Total	58.5%	67.3%	59.2%	85.8%	99.7%
All Buyers					
Canada	335	1,211	637	835	231
Total N. America	335	1,211	637	835	231
Belgium	0	11	0	0	0
Germany	20	0	0	0	0
Netherlands	6	0	0	0	0
Norway	0	0	0	15	0
United Kingdom	94	112	112	0	0
Total W. Europe	120	123	112	15	0
Estonia	7	0	0	5	0
Total E. Europe	7	0	0	5	0
Israel	0	7	7	2	0
Saudi Arabia	13	0	0	0	0
United Arab Emirates	0	0	0	2	0
Total Middle East	13	7	7	4	0
Kenya	23	0	0	0	0
South Africa	213	229	144	101	0
Total Africa	236	229	144	101	0
Hong Kong	24	0	0	186	0
India	15	0	0	0	0
Japan	123	89	51	45	1
Korea South	0	2	0	0	0
Philippines	0	2	0	0	0
Thailand	321	0	0	300	0
Vietnam	79	72	72	0	0
Total Asia	562	165	122	531	1
Australia	45	102	102	136	0
New Zealand	7	64	23	249	0
Total Pacific	52	166	125	385	0

U.S. Mustard Seed Exports April, 2014

(metric tons)

Crop Year	2011-12	2012-13	2012-13	2013-14	2014
Period	Sep-Aug	Sep-Aug	Sep-Apr	Sep-Apr	Apr
Brazil	7	23	18	3	0
Total S. America	7	23	18	3	0
Barbados	0	1	0	0	0
Costa Rica	0	0	0	7	0
Haiti	0	19	19	0	0
Mexico	224	101	101	368	87
Trinidad	0	0	0	3	0
Total C. America	224	121	120	379	87
Total World	1,554	2,045	1,284	2,259	319

Source: U.S. Department of Commerce

Australian Mustard Seed Exports April, 2014

(metric tons)

Crop Year	2011-12	2012-13	2012-13	2013-14	2014
Period	Nov-Oct	Nov-Oct	Nov-Apr	Nov-Apr	Apr
Germany	0	87	87	0	0
Netherlands	0	0	0	80	0
New Zealand	11	3	3	2	0
South Africa	2	0	0	0	0
Thailand	6	0	0	1	0
United Kingdom	2	0	0	0	0
United States	2	22	7	0	0
Total World	22	111	96	83	0

Source: Australia Bureau of Statistics

Popcorn

U.S. Popcorn Exports April, 2014
(metric tons)

Crop Year	2011-12	2012-13	2012-13	2013-14	2014
Period	Sep-Aug	Sep-Aug	Sep-Apr	Sep-Apr	Apr
Top Five Buyers					
Mexico	29,784	27,353	18,583	21,756	3,429
China	11,378	12,956	9,742	13,254	2,496
Japan	8,624	8,931	6,220	7,737	1,535
Korea South	7,997	8,557	5,672	6,287	840
United Kingdom	5,064	4,916	2,888	4,233	846
Subtotal	62,847	62,714	43,105	53,267	9,146
Percent of Total	61.4%	63.1%	62.5%	64.6%	68.4%
All Buyers					
Belgium	215	275	172	145	0
Denmark	329	471	369	242	0
Finland	179	195	156	156	39
France	683	398	378	1,092	20
Germany	484	399	298	620	40
Greece	1,577	1,070	764	821	198
Iceland	211	225	166	126	0
Ireland	804	849	564	795	223
Italy	1,068	735	561	349	83
Malta	0	0	0	21	0
Netherlands	1,219	1,023	623	1,050	124
Norway	141	62	42	256	0
Portugal	186	103	41	82	21
Spain	1,307	429	308	343	101
Sweden	1,194	1,069	745	1,151	255
Switzerland	222	222	173	112	1
United Kingdom	5,064	4,916	2,888	4,233	846
Total W. Europe	14,885	12,440	8,245	11,593	1,950

U.S. Popcorn Exports April, 2014
(metric tons)

Crop Year	2011-12	2012-13	2012-13	2013-14	2014
Period	Sep-Aug	Sep-Aug	Sep-Apr	Sep-Apr	Apr
Armenia	2	3	3	4	0
Belarus	0	20	20	0	0
Bulgaria	287	203	79	287	19
Croatia	192	191	58	267	114
Czech Republic	182	60	60	186	42
Estonia	0	0	0	21	0
Georgia	40	22	8	28	0
Hungary	301	1,791	1,153	1,090	40
Kazakhstan	0	0	0	42	0
Latvia	147	21	21	21	0
Lithuania	21	42	21	75	0
Poland	1,104	625	375	622	167
Romania	0	191	19	496	57
Russia	6,368	6,675	4,812	3,944	602
Ukraine	922	794	586	558	0
Yugoslavia	381	312	198	114	57
Total E. Europe	9,946	10,950	7,413	7,753	1,098
Bahrain	0	0	0	2	2
Cyprus	0	0	0	21	0
Egypt	61	0	0	0	0
Iraq	2	0	0	7	0
Israel	451	432	233	387	167
Jordan	95	92	60	3	0
Kuwait	15	44	34	43	23
Lebanon	69	148	131	256	21
Qatar	4	0	0	12	0
Saudi Arabia	2,130	1,506	1,302	1,309	206
Sudan	50	117	50	33	0
Turkey	132	527	527	12	0
United Arab Emirates	288	481	352	324	82
Total Middle East	3,296	3,346	2,689	2,408	501
Angola	0	0	0	41	0
Gabon	20	20	0	0	0
Mauritius	0	1	0	0	0
Morocco	3	1	0	0	0
Nigeria	36	4	3	0	0
South Africa	13	62	62	74	0
Total Africa	73	88	65	115	0

U.S. Popcorn Exports April, 2014
(metric tons)

Crop Year	2011-12	2012-13	2012-13	2013-14	2014
Period	Sep-Aug	Sep-Aug	Sep-Apr	Sep-Apr	Apr
Afghanistan	36	22	22	0	0
Bangladesh	28	0	0	14	0
Brunei Darussalam	1	2	0	21	0
China	11,378	12,956	9,742	13,254	2,496
Hong Kong	1,451	627	481	291	40
India	346	117	92	291	0
Indonesia	2,254	1,315	839	854	124
Japan	8,624	8,931	6,220	7,737	1,535
Korea South	7,997	8,557	5,672	6,287	840
Malaysia	741	780	491	657	127
Mongolia	8	8	0	25	0
Pakistan	124	355	229	285	8
Philippines	1,825	2,044	1,252	1,912	335
Singapore	429	509	356	264	0
Taiwan	1,662	1,111	815	331	19
Thailand	2,554	2,219	1,576	2,185	340
Vietnam	485	508	379	721	126
Total Asia	39,945	40,060	28,164	35,128	5,991
Australia	362	81	32	106	0
French Polynesia	0	3	3	0	0
New Zealand	158	86	64	60	19
South Georgia and the South Sandwich Islands	0	2	0	0	0
Total Pacific	520	172	98	166	19
Brazil	6	18	14	379	0
Chile	110	137	137	60	0
Colombia	736	1,117	918	1,121	273
Ecuador	1	80	64	162	0
Guyana	6	5	5	0	0
Peru	142	376	376	0	0
Suriname	4	54	17	58	0
Uruguay	10	9	0	0	0
Venezuela	17	125	108	7	0
Total S. America	1,032	1,920	1,638	1,787	273

U.S. Popcorn Exports April, 2014
(metric tons)

Crop Year	2011-12	2012-13	2012-13	2013-14	2014
Period	Sep-Aug	Sep-Aug	Sep-Apr	Sep-Apr	Apr
Bahamas	90	46	25	18	0
Barbados	40	95	65	75	15
Belize	2	4	2	17	0
Bermuda	14	15	7	11	0
Cayman Islands	2	0	0	0	0
Costa Rica	102	104	85	26	0
Dominican Republic	105	142	101	48	0
El Salvador	518	451	360	100	0
Guatemala	547	498	346	301	36
Haiti	0	0	0	1	0
Honduras	724	907	558	482	0
Jamaica	138	148	79	62	0
Leeward Windward Is.	4	10	10	5	0
Mexico	29,784	27,353	18,583	21,756	3,429
Netherlands Antilles	21	11	0	15	0
Nicaragua	202	206	146	100	0
Panama	94	141	122	185	18
Trinidad	293	310	186	248	36
Total C. America	32,678	30,441	20,674	23,448	3,534
Total World	102,374	99,416	68,987	82,398	13,366

Source: U.S. Department of Commerce

U.S. Microwave Popcorn Exports April, 2014
(metric tons)

Crop Year	2011-12	2012-13	2012-13	2013-14	2014
Period	Sep-Aug	Sep-Aug	Sep-Apr	Sep-Apr	Apr
Top Five Buyers					
Canada	30,334	33,727	22,522	24,016	3,267
Israel	1,861	1,796	1,071	906	175
Saudi Arabia	679	547	310	715	88
Costa Rica	1,045	964	585	684	88
Colombia	417	858	521	669	85
Subtotal	34,336	37,892	25,009	26,990	3,702
Percent of Total	76.1%	79.1%	78.2%	81.1%	77.0%
All Buyers					
Canada	30,334	33,727	22,522	24,016	3,267
Total N. America	30,334	33,727	22,522	24,016	3,267

U.S. Microwave Popcorn Exports April, 2014
(metric tons)

Crop Year	2011-12	2012-13	2012-13	2013-14	2014
Period	Sep-Aug	Sep-Aug	Sep-Apr	Sep-Apr	Apr
Belgium	28	10	0	7	0
Denmark	48	4	4	21	0
France	0	0	0	2	0
Germany	109	128	91	55	0
Greece	53	84	66	18	0
Iceland	173	141	74	78	3
Ireland	3	19	19	14	0
Netherlands	14	10	9	2	0
Norway	13	40	26	0	0
Portugal	1	16	9	4	0
Spain	5	5	5	6	0
Sweden	34	31	14	1	0
Switzerland	0	3	3	0	0
United Kingdom	167	117	67	79	10
Total W. Europe	648	606	387	286	13
Czech Republic	59	59	20	0	0
Georgia	0	0	0	1	0
Russia	627	402	383	93	0
Ukraine	19	60	40	40	0
Total E. Europe	706	521	443	134	0
Bahrain	21	37	27	33	7
Cyprus	11	7	7	0	0
Egypt	16	16	16	14	7
Israel	1,861	1,796	1,071	906	175
Jordan	104	148	122	95	7
Kuwait	266	276	140	241	112
Lebanon	290	278	192	238	38
Libya	0	1	0	4	3
Oman	40	27	21	20	0
Qatar	36	62	55	42	0
Saudi Arabia	679	547	310	715	88
Turkey	0	25	0	0	0
United Arab Emirates	727	652	397	503	115
Total Middle East	4,052	3,871	2,358	2,811	552

U.S. Microwave Popcorn Exports April, 2014

(metric tons)

Crop Year	2011-12	2012-13	2012-13	2013-14	2014
Period	Sep-Aug	Sep-Aug	Sep-Apr	Sep-Apr	Apr
Ghana	1	0	0	10	0
Kenya	19	17	10	9	0
Nigeria	3	2	2	8	0
South Africa	663	605	475	204	0
Tanzania	17	4	4	3	0
Zimbabwe	2	3	3	0	0
Total Africa	704	631	494	233	0
Bangladesh	0	0	0	5	0
Brunei Darussalam	2	2	2	7	2
Cambodia	0	0	0	2	0
China	379	88	53	47	3
Hong Kong	50	24	13	15	2
India	61	69	62	41	15
Indonesia	318	334	203	105	19
Japan	628	627	438	457	105
Korea South	313	561	388	399	73
Malaysia	5	12	8	4	1
Myanmar	0	10	0	0	0
Pakistan	85	93	69	36	13
Philippines	140	185	132	131	13
Singapore	60	70	49	31	7
Sri Lanka	3	6	6	0	0
Taiwan	4	21	19	7	0
Thailand	169	238	109	108	21
Vietnam	44	21	20	30	0
Total Asia	2,261	2,361	1,570	1,424	274
Australia	384	374	242	261	15
French Polynesia	34	45	30	36	12
New Zealand	700	605	474	316	32
Total Pacific	1,118	1,025	746	613	59
Bolivia	225	240	207	187	34
Brazil	1	55	34	17	0
Chile	235	118	60	93	17
Colombia	417	858	521	669	85
Ecuador	262	261	137	115	14
Guyana	0	2	2	0	0
Peru	298	247	178	188	52
Suriname	102	66	66	0	0
Uruguay	0	2	2	0	0
Venezuela	695	368	368	20	2
Total S. America	2,235	2,217	1,575	1,288	204

U.S. Microwave Popcorn Exports April, 2014

(metric tons)

Crop Year	2011-12	2012-13	2012-13	2013-14	2014
Period	Sep-Aug	Sep-Aug	Sep-Apr	Sep-Apr	Apr
Bahamas	26	26	13	14	5
Barbados	24	21	18	13	4
Belize	9	5	5	0	0
Bermuda	31	29	20	15	1
Cayman Islands	2	4	3	1	0
Costa Rica	1,045	964	585	684	88
Dominican Republic	142	186	140	94	16
El Salvador	139	137	88	129	15
Guatemala	251	309	210	249	37
Haiti	0	0	0	1	0
Honduras	36	36	26	210	48
Jamaica	57	80	57	58	7
Leeward Windward Is.	9	8	6	7	2
Mexico	675	551	337	569	157
Netherlands Antilles	21	16	12	9	1
Nicaragua	78	42	22	43	15
Panama	295	343	219	285	42
Trinidad	206	179	140	94	5
Total C. America	3,046	2,934	1,899	2,474	441
Total World	45,103	47,892	31,993	33,279	4,810

Source: U.S. Department of Commerce

Sunflower Seed

U.S. Confection Sunflower Seed Exports April, 2014
(metric tons)

Crop Year	2011-12	2012-13	2012-13	2013-14	2014
Period	Sep-Aug	Sep-Aug	Sep-Apr	Sep-Apr	Apr
Top Five Buyers					
Spain	18,094	21,091	12,672	14,537	2,128
Mexico	8,023	5,639	3,658	5,482	645
Turkey	6,874	14,757	13,050	4,803	1,724
Israel	1,746	1,993	1,298	2,326	784
Jordan	4,338	6,273	3,874	2,296	303
Subtotal	39,075	49,753	34,551	29,444	5,584
Percent of Total	67.3%	60.9%	63.3%	72.1%	82.9%
All Buyers					
Canada	809	1,227	453	1,009	127
Total N. America	809	1,227	453	1,009	127
Belgium	1,035	993	951	112	0
Denmark	26	8	8	0	0
Finland	60	0	0	0	0
France	1,256	1,108	1,034	0	0
Germany	568	159	102	278	36
Greece	1,381	1,685	942	850	58
Italy	82	41	41	60	0
Netherlands	486	1,010	890	200	0
Portugal	40	0	0	0	0
Spain	18,094	21,091	12,672	14,537	2,128
United Kingdom	196	218	180	263	37
Total W. Europe	23,222	26,312	16,820	16,300	2,260
Bulgaria	9	0	0	0	0
Czech Republic	0	0	0	1	1
Hungary	250	122	122	0	0
Poland	387	468	224	163	61
Romania	2,944	2,382	1,234	942	225
Russia	595	604	604	0	0
Ukraine	813	1,257	1,257	0	0
Total E. Europe	4,997	4,833	3,440	1,106	287

U.S. Confection Sunflower Seed Exports April, 2014

(metric tons)

Crop Year	2011-12	2012-13	2012-13	2013-14	2014
Period	Sep-Aug	Sep-Aug	Sep-Apr	Sep-Apr	Apr
Bahrain	116	253	213	97	59
Cyprus	0	141	121	0	0
Egypt	2,669	4,692	2,711	1,877	82
Iraq	0	857	857	504	143
Israel	1,746	1,993	1,298	2,326	784
Jordan	4,338	6,273	3,874	2,296	303
Kuwait	325	6,212	2,015	1,263	120
Lebanon	268	384	172	195	57
Qatar	120	141	120	159	80
Saudi Arabia	0	81	41	0	0
Syria	244	204	204	0	0
Turkey	6,874	14,757	13,050	4,803	1,724
United Arab Emirates	991	1,464	955	367	0
Total Middle East	17,691	37,450	25,628	13,887	3,352
Algeria	0	0	0	20	0
Morocco	756	1,408	979	607	0
Senegal	0	7	7	0	0
Tunisia	260	182	162	142	0
Total Africa	1,015	1,597	1,148	769	0
China	1,102	645	645	20	0
Indonesia	0	1,692	1,184	670	0
Japan	276	446	364	162	0
Korea South	81	209	133	496	17
Malaysia	0	6	0	5	1
Pakistan	0	20	20	0	0
Philippines	20	27	27	31	9
Singapore	55	0	0	0	0
Taiwan	453	604	525	217	20
Vietnam	0	126	0	104	0
Total Asia	1,987	3,773	2,897	1,705	47

U.S. Confection Sunflower Seed Exports April, 2014

(metric tons)

Crop Year	2011-12	2012-13	2012-13	2013-14	2014
Period	Sep-Aug	Sep-Aug	Sep-Apr	Sep-Apr	Apr
Argentina	0	36	36	0	0
Brazil	9	0	0	0	0
Chile	0	53	39	13	0
Colombia	13	0	0	8	0
Ecuador	202	783	431	554	19
Total S. America	225	872	506	576	19
Costa Rica	61	20	20	0	0
El Salvador	0	3	0	0	0
Mexico	8,023	5,639	3,658	5,482	645
Trinidad	0	20	20	0	0
Total C. America	8,084	5,682	3,699	5,482	645
Total World	58,032	81,746	54,591	40,834	6,736

Source: U.S. Department of Commerce

U.S. Hulled Sunflower Seed Exports April, 2014

(metric tons)

Crop Year	2011-12	2012-13	2012-13	2013-14	2014
Period	Sep-Aug	Sep-Aug	Sep-Apr	Sep-Apr	Apr
Top Five Buyers					
Canada	5,701	3,762	2,567	2,220	346
Spain	2,156	1,909	1,206	1,632	68
Mexico	1,633	1,044	630	595	70
Korea South	818	1,176	533	581	137
Germany	476	294	159	456	91
Subtotal	10,783	8,185	5,095	5,483	712
Percent of Total	64.6%	65.5%	66.1%	77.4%	87.5%
All Buyers					
Canada	5,701	3,762	2,567	2,220	346
Total N. America	5,701	3,762	2,567	2,220	346

U.S. Hulled Sunflower Seed Exports April, 2014
(metric tons)

Crop Year Period	2011-12 Sep-Aug	2012-13 Sep-Aug	2012-13 Sep-Apr	2013-14 Sep-Apr	2014 Apr
Belgium	190	18	0	0	0
Denmark	38	0	0	0	0
Finland	139	0	0	0	0
Germany	476	294	159	456	91
Greece	120	319	299	0	0
Italy	0	76	56	0	0
Netherlands	35	8	8	37	0
Norway	105	0	0	0	0
Spain	2,156	1,909	1,206	1,632	68
United Kingdom	1,356	573	292	100	37
Total W. Europe	4,614	3,198	2,020	2,223	196
Estonia	57	0	0	0	0
Romania	458	222	154	138	0
Total E. Europe	515	222	154	138	0
Bahrain	167	0	0	0	0
Cyprus	20	19	0	0	0
Egypt	520	301	161	0	0
Israel	837	827	425	165	18
Kuwait	113	40	0	0	0
Lebanon	98	0	0	0	0
Saudi Arabia	0	206	83	0	0
Turkey	138	609	571	40	0
United Arab Emirates	1	130	43	20	0
Total Middle East	1,894	2,131	1,283	225	18
Kenya	0	0	0	2	0
Morocco	39	0	0	155	0
Tunisia	0	22	22	0	0
Total Africa	39	22	22	158	0
China	55	18	18	229	0
Hong Kong	0	1	0	0	0
Indonesia	0	365	0	223	0
Japan	387	84	68	225	18
Korea South	818	1,176	533	581	137
Malaysia	154	104	45	102	0
Philippines	99	29	29	0	0
Singapore	202	153	153	73	18
Taiwan	43	20	20	9	0

U.S. Hulled Sunflower Seed Exports April, 2014

(metric tons)

Crop Year	2011-12	2012-13	2012-13	2013-14	2014
Period	Sep-Aug	Sep-Aug	Sep-Apr	Sep-Apr	Apr
Total Asia	1,757	1,950	866	1,442	173
Australia	116	37	37	18	0
Total Pacific	116	37	37	18	0
Brazil	0	0	0	4	0
Chile	95	0	0	42	8
Colombia	17	18	18	0	0
Ecuador	313	110	104	19	2
Total S. America	425	128	122	65	10
El Salvador	0	0	0	1	0
Guatemala	0	10	6	0	0
Mexico	1,633	1,044	630	595	70
Trinidad	1	0	0	1	1
Total C. America	1,635	1,054	636	597	71
Total World	16,697	12,504	7,705	7,085	814

Source: U.S. Department of Commerce

Other Specialty Crops

Buckwheat

Canadian Buckwheat Supply and Demand Estimates
(metric tons, acres)

Year	2010	2011	2012	2013	2014
Acreage	4,216	5,081	11,535	6,300	5,700
Yield (pounds)	837	824	803	805	812
Production (MT)	1,600	1,900	4,200	2,300	2,100
Imports	1,633	1,553	1,072	1,600	1,000
Carryin	2,600	2,000	200	225	100
Stocks	5,833	5,453	5,472	4,125	3,200
Disappearance					
Aug-Apr Exports	2,116	3,715	2,858	2,930	N/A
Percent of Forecast	90.2 %	90.8 %	75.7 %	88.8 %	N/A
Total Export	2,345	4,091	3,775	3,300	2,000
Seed & Waste	230	490	505	300	401
Domestic	1,259	672	967	425	599
Usage	3,834	5,253	5,247	4,025	3,000
Carryover	2,000	200	225	100	200
Usage/Stocks	52.2 %	3.8 %	4.3 %	2.5 %	6.7 %

Forecasts by STAT Market Research based on data from Statistics Canada

Australian Buckwheat Exports April, 2014
(metric tons)

Crop Year	2011-12	2012-13	2012-13	2013-14	2014
Period	Nov-Oct	Nov-Oct	Nov-Apr	Nov-Apr	Apr
Indonesia	0	0	0	2	0
Japan	327	48	0	0	0
New Zealand	18	18	1	26	6
Singapore	9	37	12	3	0
Thailand	9	0	0	5	0
Total World	363	104	14	36	6

Source: Australia Bureau of Statistics

Canadian Buckwheat Exports April, 2014

(metric tons)

Crop Year	2011-12	2012-13	2012-13	2013-14	2014
Period	Aug-Jul	Aug-Jul	Aug-Apr	Aug-Apr	Apr
Falkland Islands	73	0	0	0	0
France	288	1,160	600	798	81
Hong Kong	0	0	0	6	0
Italy	0	12	12	0	0
Japan	1,476	258	258	25	25
United Kingdom	28	22	22	13	0
United States	2,227	2,322	1,965	2,089	649
Total World	4,091	3,775	2,858	2,930	756

Source: Statistics Canada

U.S. Buckwheat Exports April, 2014

(metric tons)

Crop Year	2011-12	2012-13	2012-13	2013-14	2014
Period	Sep-Aug	Sep-Aug	Sep-Apr	Sep-Apr	Apr
Australia	0	9	9	0	0
Canada	536	767	464	363	15
China	0	8,321	0	0	0
Dominican Republic	6	57	57	0	0
France	0	5	5	0	0
Israel	0	60	60	0	0
Japan	27,803	17,103	13,943	8,846	1,160
Netherlands Antilles	10	0	0	0	0
Portugal	0	40	0	0	0
South Africa	0	3	3	0	0
Sweden	169	79	79	0	0
Taiwan	76	2	0	2	0
Thailand	0	42	42	42	21
Total World	28,600	26,486	14,662	9,252	1,196

Source: U.S. Department of Commerce

Vetch and Lupins

Australian Lupin Supply and Demand Estimates
(metric tons, acres)

Year	2010	2011	2012	2013	2014
Acreage	1,403,281	1,702,519	1,112,444	955,906	1,079,827
Yield (lbs)	965	1,166	909	1,441	1,132
Production	614,400	900,550	458,700	625,000	554,700
Carry In	24,000	34,000	18,000	17,000	52,000
Stocks	638,400	934,550	476,700	642,000	606,700
Disappearance					
Export	186,000	500,000	175,000	306,000	277,000
Seed	139,000	91,000	78,000	88,000	88,000
Feed & Other	279,400	325,550	206,700	196,000	215,700
Total Usage	604,400	916,550	459,700	590,000	580,700
Ending Stock	34,000	18,000	17,000	52,000	26,000
Stocks/Use	5.6 %	2.0 %	3.7 %	8.8 %	4.5 %

Forecasts by STAT Market Research based on data from ABARE, ABS and Pulse Australia

Australian Vetch and Forage Exports April, 2014

(metric tons)

Crop Year	2011-12	2012-13	2012-13	2013-14	2014
Period	Nov-Oct	Nov-Oct	Nov-Apr	Nov-Apr	Apr
Top Five Buyers					
United States	214	378	290	715	227
Taiwan	211	67	45	399	0
Philippines	501	542	347	357	0
Belgium	470	788	674	338	97
United Kingdom	546	190	190	311	0
Subtotal	1,943	1,964	1,545	2,120	324
Percent of Total	10.6%	40.7%	60.5%	84.5%	81.0%
All Buyers					
United States	214	378	290	715	227
Total N. America	214	378	290	715	227
Belgium	470	788	674	338	97
France	624	26	22	22	0
Germany	0	129	65	22	0
Italy	12,261	762	184	96	0
Netherlands	217	250	204	0	0
Portugal	93	90	45	5	0
Spain	281	182	182	0	0
Switzerland	0	60	60	100	0
United Kingdom	546	190	190	311	0
Total W. Europe	14,492	2,476	1,624	892	97
Bahrain	71	43	0	0	0
Jordan	264	23	23	0	0
Kuwait	47	0	0	0	0
Saudi Arabia	20	0	0	0	0
Turkey	1,021	68	68	0	0
Total Middle East	1,423	134	91	0	0
South Africa	4	63	43	10	0
Total Africa	4	63	43	10	0
Japan	312	303	116	86	40
Korea South	1,113	860	0	41	36
Philippines	501	542	347	357	0
Taiwan	211	67	45	399	0
Total Asia	2,137	1,771	507	883	76
Argentina	60	0	0	0	0
Uruguay	0	0	0	8	0
Total S. America	60	0	0	8	0
Total World	18,331	4,821	2,554	2,509	400

Source: Australia Bureau of Statistics

www.ingramcontent.com/pod-product-compliance
Lightning Source LLC
LaVergne TN
LVHW070951210926
848482LV00002B/175